KEEP LOOKING UP

Sermons on the Psalms

C. Anthony Hunt

TABLE OF CONTENTS

Acknowledgements

Over the course of my faith journey, I have grown to love the Book of Psalms. I love preaching, teaching, praying and living the psalms. For me, they have become my songs, speaking to the joys and sorrows, pleasure and pain, smiles and tears, praise and possibility of life. Indeed, as was the case with the ancient Israelites, these songs speak to every thread of the fabric and texture of the lives that we live.

The sermons contained in this volume speak to the various and sundry vicissitudes of life - our striving towards God, our need for comfort and encouragement, and our reasons to celebrate the goodness of God. Importantly, the volume's title, *Keep Looking Up,* speaks to the hope to which we as people of faith are called – that amidst what may often appear to be insurmountable odds and obstacles, we are called to look to God as the source of our strength.

I take this opportunity to first offer thanks and praise to God who is the source of my strength, the strength of my life, and the one to whom I perpetually look for help, and in whom I find it. I thank my immediate family – my wife Lisa, and our children, Kristen, Brian and Marcus (deceased) – for their consistent love, patience and encouragement at every juncture of life. To my parents, grandparents, and all of my extended family, I am forever grateful for all that we have and continue to share. I dedicate this volume to my father, William Delaney Hunt, who embodies all that is contained in this volume.

To the people of Epworth Chapel United Methodist Church, Baltimore, MD where I am now blessed to serve as pastor, and to St. Mary's Seminary and University, the Graduate Theological Foundation and Wesley Theological Seminary, where

I am privileged to teach, and to all of the places I have been privileged to serve in ministry over the past 25 years, I am grateful to each of you for sharing with me on the faith journey, as we have co-joined in the preaching, teaching and living of these and other psalms.

My prayer is that this volume – which contains 22 sermons on the psalms - will be a blessing and encouragement to all of us on life's journey, and that we will all find hope in God, and continue in all that we do to "keep looking up!"

Section One
Songs of Ascent

Chapter 1
KEEP LOOKING UP

I lift my eyes to the hills – from where will my help come? My help comes from the Lord, who made heaven and earth. (Psalm 121:1-2)

A number of years ago, the great soul singing group "Earth, Wind and Fire" sang a song that offered words of encouragement to their listeners when they sang:

"Keep your head to the sky."

Indeed these are days when we all need to be encouraged to look beyond ourselves, beyond our present circumstances, beyond the various ups and downs of life to better days that are ahead.

"Keep your head to the sky."

These are words that encourage us to keep our heads up, to hang in there regardless of the vicissitudes that are bound to come our way – and to keep looking up.

These are very trying times in which we live. The newspapers are littered with accounts of bad and discouraging news. It seems that hopelessness abounds, and that there is not much joy to be found.

Philosopher Cornel West has referred to the present condition of our society as "nihilism." A certain nothingness, meaninglessness, lovelessness and apparent hopelessness seem to exist among people today.

Indeed, life can take strange and often difficult twists. We will all be dealt difficult blows that serve to knock us down, put us down, and keep us down. People who we may have thought to be trustworthy will let us down. And it is in these instances that we may be tempted to put our heads down, throw in the towel, and give up on life.

This is one reason why the rate of depression is so high throughout our society today. Many people are down and out. Suicide rates are higher than they have ever been, among virtually all groups of people, because so many people have become so down on life that they see no reason to look to tomorrow.

And amidst all of this, we who are people who walk by faith and not by sight look for answers and meaning in the presence of God. Somebody has declared that "If we've ever needed the Lord before, we sure do need God now."

I believe that it was at his point of most profound need that the psalmist spoke here in Psalm 121. The psalmist was on a journey and he needed a song of hope to encourage him in knowing that God was with him. Regarding his search for God – he asked this familiar question:

"I look to the hills, from whence cometh my help?"

As we look closely at this text, I believe we can sense that the psalmist was dealing with the matter of feeling Godforsaken. He was speaking from a point of his own desperate search for the Lord. He was pondering a serious matter here.

"Where is God when I need God? Where is my help when I need it?" The psalmist was going through some things on his journey, and he needed to know who he could put his trust in and depend on. He had searched, and he needed to identify his help – the psalmist needed to identify the source of his strength and the strength of his life in these moments of despair and God forsakenness. He was at the end of his rope – and he needed to know where he could find his help.

Many of us can relate to the predicament of the psalmist. Have you ever been there - looking, searching, yearning, pondering, waiting and wondering where the Lord was when you needed God the most?

"I looked the hills, from whence cometh my help?"

One of the precarious predicaments for Christians is rooted in how we are to deal with the times in life when things aren't going our way. How are we supposed to cope in times when we feel alone, separated, alienated and weak? What are we to do when it seems that God is the hardest to find?

We hear that Christ died for us, but we can't seem to get through the death situations of our life. We sing and declare "what a friend we have in Jesus" – and then there are times when we really feel friendless. We hear the promise of Jesus to his disciples: "I will never leave you or forsake you" – and yet we feel all alone.

If you know like I know, it often becomes difficult to keep our heads up, and to keep pressing on and moving on in life. God where are you when I need you the most?

The songwriter wrote of this despair in a song -
> I cried and I cried, I cried all night long,
> I cried and I cried, until I found the Lord.
> I just couldn't rest contented,
> Until I found the Lord.

> I moaned and I moaned, I moaned all night long,
> I moaned and I moaned, until I found the Lord…

The psalmist would end this short section of his lament in Psalm 121 with an affirmation of his faith:
> *"My help comes from the Lord."*

Indeed, as he searched, his question as to the existence of his help became an affirmation of faith with an answer – *"I know that my help comes from the Lord."*

As we hear of the experience of the psalmist, the word for us is to keep looking up!

Why do we need to keep looking up? What are the benefits for us to keep looking up?

First, as we look up we realize that God never lets us down. *(God won't let you down.)*   It has been declared that God sits high and looks low. The songwriter wrote words that encourage us:
> Father I stretch my hands to thee,
> No other help I know,
> If thou withdraw thyself from me,
> Where will I go?

The psalmist would declare at another point that:
> *"Though my mother and father forsake me,*
> *I know the Lord is there to take me in."*

It's good to know that God won't let us down. Friends and even family members might not always come through when you need them, but God won't let you down.

Second, when we look up, we realize that God never leaves us alone. *(God won't leave us alone.)* God is always with us. David said, *"I've been young and I've been old, yet I've never seen the righteous forsaken, or his seed begging for bread."* (Psalm 37:25)

It has been written:
> There's not a friend like the lowly Jesus,
> No not one, no not one,
> There's not a moment that he does not cheer us,
> No not one, no not one.
> Jesus knows all about our struggles,
> He won't rest till the day is done.
> There's not a friend like the lowly Jesus,
> No not one, no not one.

If you hang in there, God will be there for you.

Third, as we look up, we realize that God knows what we need. *(God will provide.)* It has been declared that "God never sleeps and God never slumbers. God watches us both day and night." We look up with eyes of faith believing that God knows what we need, and is able to provide for all of our needs. God can and God will provide for us.

I've come to remind us that whatever we need, God has it.
> If you need more joy, God has it.
> If you need peace, God has it.

If you need hope, God has it!

We are encouraged to keep looking up!

As we think about Jesus, we realize that the Lord kept looking up.

- Though Satan tried to tempt the Lord, he kept looking up to God his father.
- Though the same people that the Lord would help, would "'buke him and scorn him", the Lord kept looking up.
- Though his enemies hung him on a cross to die a crucified death, Jesus kept looking up.

And we likewise need to keep looking up today. For when we look up, we realize that God is bigger than our biggest problem.
God's so high you can't get over him,
So low you can't get under him,
So wide you can't get around him!

Keep looking up…

I'm glad that our help is in the Lord.

Over my head, I hear music in the air,
Over my head, I hear music in the air,
There must be a God somewhere!

Chapter 2
THEY COULDN'T KEEP ME (US) DOWN!

Often they have attacked me from my youth, yet they have not prevailed against me. (Psalm 129:2)

In ancient times, the Book of Psalms essentially served as a primary worship resource for the Jewish community. It was their hymn book – their hymnal - as the community gathered in tabernacles, the Temple and later in synagogues to extol the holiness and goodness of their God.

The Book of Psalms contains a number of different literary types - all of which relate to and speak to the spiritual life of the people of Israel. Biblical scholars have pointed out that the Psalter can be divided into at least five different major categories - (1) Songs of Praise, (2) Songs of Individual Lament, (3) Songs of Community Lament, (4) Songs for Royal Observance, and (5) Songs of Thanksgiving.

These various categories of songs spoke to the plethora of real life conditions – everyday realities that confronted the Israelites. In Psalms 120 through 134, we find what are also referred to as Songs of Ascent. This sub-group of songs is among those that the Israelites would sing as they made their way from the low ground up to Jerusalem. As they participated in their upward climb toward Zion, it was customary for them to sing such Songs of Ascent. These songs served as a form of encouragement, strength and hope as they pressed their way on the long, upward pilgrim journey to Zion.

We recall that the Israelites were a wandering people. From the time of Abraham through all of the generations that followed, Israel had wandered - finding refuge not always in a defined space or place, but often finding solace and hope in God wherever they found themselves. Over centuries, this community of pilgrim people had learned to travel, and wherever they found themselves on the journey they knew that God was present with them. In their traveling – in this sojourning - they had learned to trust in the God of their fathers and mothers:

> ♦ Whether within the confines of 430 years of bondage in Egypt, or at the banks of the Red Sea - they had learned how to trust God.
>
> ♦ Whether they were wandering in the wilderness, or standing at the brink of the Promised Land at the Jordan River - they had learned how to trust God.
>
> ♦ Whether they found themselves at home in Jerusalem or in exile in Babylon - they had learned how to trust their God.

It was their songs - like this one that we find in Psalm 129 - that had sustained and nurtured their faith on the journey. It was their songs of faith - their songs of Zion - that served to remind them in moments of doubt and wonder of the trust that their forebears had placed in God, and how God had kept them and never left them over the years…how God had provided for all of their needs.

Here in Psalm 129, the psalmist takes time to recall some of the difficulties of their journey. The psalmist declares that *"Often have they attacked me from my youth, yet they have not prevailed against me."*

Here, the psalmist gives a personal account of what he had gone through, as perhaps a way of helping others on the journey, and he says essentially – *"Whatever they tried to do to me - they could not keep me down."*

Why is it important that we deal with this psalm today? How does the psalmist's affirmation speak to you and me at this moment?

This particular song is important because it speaks to the persistent nature of difficulties in life. This psalm speaks first to the inevitable and pervasive nature of the adversaries and adversities that people of faith will face. This psalm speaks of struggles, of trials and tribulations that we will all face.

If you know like I know, we will all face challenges in our lives. Storms will come in like a flood. Difficulties and disappointments are a part of the raw material of life. Night will come, and often seem to endure for too long. In the midst of it all, we will need to rest in the assurance that God is still real, and more importantly, that God is present in the midst of our troubles.

We need to hear this psalm today because trouble will come our way, and disappointment is bound to meet us and greet us in particular and personal ways.

Trouble is bound to meet us and greet us in our homes, on our jobs, at school, and even at church. Trouble lurks with loved ones, with friends, with adversaries and enemies. Trouble is in our way with racism, and sexism, and militarism, and classism, and with drugs and violence all around us.

But in the midst of these struggles, the psalmist speaks of the goodness, grace and providence of God. Through it all - God had been with him. Through many dangers, toils and snares - God had remained perpetually present as his strength and his shield.

In his song, the psalmist offers us some words of encouragement and hope. He was saying that "whenever, and wherever, and however my enemies tried to attack me - they could not keep me down."

Indeed, we need to know that the Christian stance in the midst of opposition and despair is one of hope. A war rages between hope and despair in the heart of every believer from time to time, but our lives must be animated with hope - lest we lose courage.

♦ When our lives are animated with hope - we can face opposition with confidence and faith.

♦ When we are animated with hope - we can stand amidst all of those things and persons that try to knock us down.

♦ When we have hope - we can mount up with wings as eagles…run and not get weary…walk and not faint.

Indeed, the psalmist offers us some words of encouragement and hope. *"Often they have attacked me from my youth, but they could not keep me down."*

But despite these strong and confident words - some of you might be like me, and have some doubts and reservations every now and then. So I had to look somewhere else to make sure (be certain) that the psalmist was not just speaking of some "pie in the sky" notion of a God somewhere "over there".

So I consulted the chief psalmist, David at another place. I looked at David's life, and I realized that through all that David went through, he was able to keep on singing - keep on hoping - and keep on affirming the goodness of the Lord.

♦ In the midst of his troubles, David said, *"I will bless the Lord at all times. God's praise shall continually be in my mouth."* (Psalm 34:1)

♦ In the midst of his loneliness, David declared, *"The Lord is my shepherd, and I shall not want."* (Psalm 23:1)

♦ In the midst of his midnight hour, David affirmed that *"Weeping may endure for a night, but joy comes in the morning."* (Psalm 30:5)

♦ And as he looked back over his own life, David declared that *"I've been young, and I've been old, yet I've never seen the righteous forsaken, or his seed begging for bread."* (Psalm 37:25)

But even David's strong faith might not be enough to convince and convict you of the goodness of God when the adversary tries to take you out.

So maybe it would help us to also think on Jesus:

♦ They tell me that his adversaries hung him high on an old rugged cross...

♦ The Lord hung there for three long hours...

♦ Then they took him down, and put him in an old borrowed tomb...

♦ As the Lord lay there for two days, his adversaries thought they had him down...

♦ But on the third day (early on Sunday morning), Jesus rose from the dead!

I've come to remind us that Jesus got up, so that you and I could get up!

I can declare, as I believe the psalmist could declare, that "When I look back over my life, and think things over, I can truly say that I've been blessed... I've got a testimony." And I know

I'm not alone. In other words, they tried, but they could not keep me (us) down!

- ♦   They tried every trick in the book, but they could not keep us down!

- ♦   They said we wouldn't make it, but I'm here to tell you that they could not keep us down!

I was sinking deep in sin
Far from the peaceful shore…
Very deeply stained within
Sinking to rise no more…
But the master of the sea
Heard my despairing cry…
From the water
Lifted me
Now safe am I.
Love lifted me… Love lifted me.
When nothing else would help
Love lifted me!

Chapter 3
IT'S GOOD TO BE HERE

I was glad when they said to me, "Let us go into the house of the Lord!" Our feet are standing within your gates, O Jerusalem. (Psalm 122:1-2)

These are days when there are some of those among us who question the very reality of God, let alone the necessity of the church. Why do people today need the Lord? What relevance does the church have for our lives today?

Many people live under the false illusions and misguided premises that they have all that they need in the world, and that they don't have any need for God in their lives. Many people have been blessed to receive a good education, attain a decent job, and live in a comfortable home, and might have cause to wonder what in the world it is that God and the church can do for them.

You know how many people are. God is a God of convenience for us – a kind of "7-11" God - who we think we can just stop by and pick something up from when we need it. Many people only call on God when we need something from the Lord – as though the Lord is a divine bellhop – at our beck and call when we find ourselves in need:

- We don't pray unless we need a breakthrough.

- We don't go to Bible study unless we know that we need a revelation.

- We don't come to church until we know that we need a blessing.

- We don't even praise God unless we expect a blessing to come down for us.

And lest you think I'm misguided in my observation, just check out the shopping malls late on any Sunday morning. Just drive by the neighborhood soccer or lacrosse fields, or stop by the gym or the golf course on any Sunday morning, or go by the restaurants that offer Sunday brunch, and you're likely to find quite a few people – even some who consider themselves to be Christians and church members - who don't (or no longer) think they have any need for God or the church in their lives.

Just check out the number of people (even church members) who choose to regularly sleep in on Sunday mornings, or tailgate at football games, or go to the beach, or to amusement parks, and we'll find quite a few people who don't (or no longer) think they need God, or the church.

And lest we think these challenges are unique to the contemporary age, let us be reminded that the context in which the psalmist addresses the people of faith here in Psalm 122 is similar to what we face today. The psalmist declares *"I was glad when they said unto me, "Let us go into the house of the Lord.""*

This was a song of ascent. The Israelites had been marching to Zion – they had been pressing their way up to Jerusalem – they had been climbing up to the house of the Lord, where they expected that they would meet God. And as a part of their affirmation of faith in God, they would sing their songs – songs of Zion – songs like:

- *"I looked to hills from whence cometh my help? My help comes from the Lord."* (121:1)
- *"How very good and pleasant it is for sisters and brothers to dwell together in unity."* (133:1)

- *"If it had not been for the Lord who was on my side, where would I be?"* (124:1)

These Songs of Ascent were their songs – songs that encouraged them to press on to see what the end would be, songs that reminded them of the very presence, provision and power of God. These were songs that helped them remember that if God had blessed them before, God could and would do it again. And so as they made their way to Zion, the psalmist was leading the people of God in song, and letting those of his day know that he not only wanted to go into God's house, but he was glad to get there. There's something to be said of not only getting to the Lord's house, but being glad to get here:

- Glad to get here, because we know that God is in the house,
- Glad to get here, because this is where God's people are,
- Glad to get here, because we know that when we get to God's house, God is going to do something to change our lives.

"I was glad when they said to me let us go to the Lord's house."

That's' why I've come to declare that *it's good to be here* today. I realize that some of us may have had other things to do today – some may have come to church begrudgingly – some may not have felt like coming – some may have come because they were dragged to church by somebody else - but if you're like me – you can declare now that we're here, that it's good to be here.

As I have grown older, there are a few important things that I have come to realize and appreciate about how I was raised. One of those things is that I realize now that growing up, I had a "drug" problem. You see, my parents and grandparents "drug" (dragged) me to church, and they "drug" (dragged) me to Sunday school, and they "drug" (dragged) me to youth group, and they "drug" (dragged) me to choir rehearsal.

It's good to be here – because –
- If we hadn't made it here, we would not have known fully of the presence of the Lord.
- If we hadn't made it here, we wouldn't realize that when we couldn't pray for ourselves, somebody prayed for us, and had us on their mind.
- If we hadn't made it here, we wouldn't have been reminded again that Jesus died for you and for me.
- If we hadn't made it into the house of the Lord, we might have forgotten the power of praise.
- If we hadn't made it here, we may not have been reminded that God is Good, and the Lord is Good all the time!

It's good to be here today!

Chapter 4
SAY SO

O give thanks to the Lord for God is good; for God's steadfast love endures forever. Let the redeemed of the Lord say so... *(Psalm 107:1-2a.)*

Lest you are wondering who this sermon is directed toward, I want to begin by letting you know that this sermon is for the redeemed. No, this is not really a sermon for those who are searching, or questioning, or still trying to find God – this sermon is for the redeemed. This is not a sermon for those who may harbor doubt about the presence and power of God – nor is it for those who are unsure about their relationship with the Lord. This is a sermon for the redeemed.

The words of the psalmist are a clarion call to all of us who have been blessed to be redeemed by God. It is a word for all of us who know that God has claimed our lives and changed us from whom and what we used to be. The psalmist says, *"Let the redeemed of the Lord say so."*

In this the information age, it seems that words flow more freely than ever across any number of media. Ours is the age of the Internet, and cable television. This is the age of High Definition and Blue Ray technology. It is the age of Blue Tooth, the Blackberry, Twitter, Apple, the IPad, the IPod and the IPhone. It is the age of instant messaging and text messaging – of YouTube and Facebook and Instagram. We live in a time of twenty-four hour news cycles, where news – good news, bad news, any kind of news - seems to pervade the airwaves and inundate our collective conscience. This is an age where words seem to abound.

The psalmist here offers the challenge to the redeemed of the Lord to "say so." He says, *"O give thanks to the Lord, for God is good, God's steadfast love endures forever. Let the redeemed of the Lord say so, those God redeemed from trouble and gathered from the lands, from the east and the west, from the north and the south."*

These are words of thanksgiving for how the Lord has delivered him (and others) from times of trouble. The psalmist first reminds us that we ought to *give thanks, for the Lord is good.* This speaks to the omni-benevolence of God. We have become accustomed in the church today to declaring that "God is good… all the time, and all the time… God is good."

The psalmist wanted us to know that the goodness of God was evident in his life. He wanted those who would hear his song to know that the Lord had been good to him.

I'm sure that if we took a moment to reflect, we too could also attest to the goodness of the Lord. When we were sick, God healed us. When we were in need, God made a way. When we were in trouble, the Lord came to see about us.

And because of the goodness of the Lord, because of who God is and what the Lord has done, the psalmist wanted to encourage redeemed people to say so.

I realize that it might be difficult for some of us to declare what God has done in our lives. I know that somebody is saying, "I'm not a preacher, nor am I an evangelist. You're asking me to go outside my comfort zone, and do something God has not called me to do, or equipped me to do." We need to know that we are not alone - many in the Bible could attest to the challenge incumbent in the call of the psalmist to "say so":

- Moses was a stammering, stuttering murderer - and God called him to lead the people of Israel out of slavery and toward the Promised Land.
- Jonah was a reluctant, resistant preacher - and God redeemed him, saved him and turned him around from his waywardness, and sent him to Nineveh to preach revival.
- Job lost just about everything that was important to him - and after all that he went through, God restored him, and he was able to declare, *"I know that my redeemer lives."*
- Saul was traveling on a Damascus road – on his way to persecute Christians – and God knocked him down, blinded him, turned his life around, and changed his name to Paul.

Perhaps, it is the life of Paul that helps us the most to understand what the psalmist was saying when he said, *"Let the redeemed of the Lord say so."* Paul knew something about redemption:

- That's why Paul could declare that we have *"been bought with a price"*. (1 Corinthians 6:20)
- That's why he could declare that *"If any person is in Christ Jesus he or she is a new creation..."* (2 Corinthians 5:17)
- That is why he could encourage us to *"Be not conformed to this world, but be transformed by the renewing of our minds."* (Romans 12:2)
- That's why Paul could declare that he was *"not ashamed of the gospel of Jesus Christ for it is the power of God... for those who believe."* (Romans 1:16) Paul knew something about being redeemed.

These words about being redeemed - and saying so - should lead us to think about what God has done in our lives. They should lead us to count our blessings and name them one-by-one.

We need to know and be able to declare that God is a God of redemption. The late theologian Olin Moyd wrote of this in his book, *Redemption in Black Theology,* and pointed out that redemption is the vital core of Black theology, and that as we are redeemed by God we are not only "delivered from something", but when we are redeemed, we are "accepted into something." Indeed, redemption means that you and I have been accepted into the kin-dom, the family of God, and into all of God's goodness.

When thinking about redemption and what Christ has done in my life, I remember how in days past, my grandmother collected S&H Green Stamps when she bought things from the grocery store. As she collected green stamps, she would put them in her stamp book. When my grandmother had collected enough stamps, she would then take them to the store to exchange them – to redeem the stamps - for a special household item that she had been wanting and waiting to have.

Ultimately, that is what Christ has done for us. Christ came into the world, and has entered into our lives to be our redemption, to buy us back, and claim us for God. What the psalmist was really trying to tell us is that if we know we've been redeemed, we ought to have a testimony:

> - A testimony – When God blesses us, we should be willing and able (glad) to let somebody else know what the Lord has done for us.
> - A testimony – "I said I wasn't gone tell nobody, but I just couldn't keep it to myself."

Why should we have a testimony (what are the benefits of a testimony)?

- First, our testimony lets God know that we are thankful for what the Lord has done for us.
- Second, our testimony can help somebody else who is going through something know of the goodness of the Lord. We're really blessed to be a blessing. We're not alone - we're in this thing called life together. As the song says: "There is no limit to what God can do - what God has done for others – God will do the same for (me and) you…
- Third, our testimony gets us ready for our next blessing. David said, *"I will bless the Lord at all times, God's praise shall continually be in my mouth."* We are reminded in scripture that the Lord *inhabits the praises of those who bow down before him.*

The psalmist reminds us that we need to "say so." God has claimed us, and then God has renamed us -

- Say so… we were sinners, but now we're saved!
- Say so… we were bound, but now we're free!
- Say so… we were lost, but now we're found!
- Say so… we were blind, but now we see!

Say so!
Amazing grace…
How sweet the sound
That saved a wretch like me.
I once was lost
But now I'm found
Was blind, but now I see!   (John Newton, "Amazing Grace")

Chapter 5
OBEY YOUR THIRST

> **My soul thirsts for God, for the living God. When shall I come and behold the face of God? (Psalm 42:2)**

In the scripture text from Psalm 42, we find that the writer is one who is obviously yearning for a closer relationship with God. He is seeking and searching for something more, something deeper in his spiritual walk. And so he begins this psalm abruptly with the metaphor of a thirsty, panting deer. The deer is frantically searching in the desert for a stream of water.

With the same intensity as the deer seeks water, the psalmist seeks after God. He declares, *"My soul thirsts for God, for the living God."* He is speaking to a need that is common among all of us. An integral part of the human plight is a need to know God and to experience God. This is what St. Augustine spoke of in his prayer, "Lord you have created us for yourself, and our souls are restless until they find their rest in thee." All of us in some way have souls that are restless and thirsty for the Lord.

Here, the psalmist offers the image of a deer that is thirsty. And although the psalmist points to the deer's longing in the midst of physical thirst and danger, this metaphor offers a profound spiritual image - our relationship with God is as essential to our spiritual well-being as water is to our physical well-being.

Growing up, my paternal grandparents lived across the road from a well. I can remember playing outside their house in the hot summer sun, and there would come a point when we knew that it was time to stop playing, for we were thirsty.

We knew that it was time to go to the well, and pump it until water started to gush out.   We'd pump and pump, and there was nothing like the sight of seeing water start to flow out of the well, and nothing like knowing that our thirst would then be quenched.

Indeed, all of us have found ourselves at the point of being thirsty. Being thirsty places us at the point of needing to address one of the basic necessities of life. The fact is that we can't survive without water. Without water we would die. It has been suggested that thirst is such a powerful longing that it displaces all other human desires.

This image of being thirsty may be lost on some of us in a day and age when there is so much that substitutes for the basic elements of life. Even knowing what we thirst for – what we need most essentially in our lives - is often lost amidst the plethora of things that grasp our attention and seek to satisfy our needs.

In reflecting on the matter of being thirsty, I recalled hearing the phrase "Obey Your Thirst" in a television commercial from some time ago.   And so, not having paid full attention, I asked my daughter which company used the slogan, thinking it was Gatorade. She insisted that it wasn't Gatorade, but that it was Sprite. I insisted that I thought the slogan belonged to Gatorade.

So in this age of "googling," my daughter suggested that we "google" the phrase to see which of us was right. Our Google search proved that my daughter was right – it was not Gatorade – it was Sprite. "Obey Your Thirst."

In this contemporary and commercial age, many forms of beverage have emerged that claim to be thirst quenchers. Just go into the store and you will find on the shelves any number of so-called thirst quenching products. There's flavored water, vitamin water, Gatorade, PowerAde, and any number of other products. But, there's still something that leads me to believe that none of these really takes the place of water itself.

We've now even bought into the bottled water explosion. It is now a multi-billion dollar, global phenomenon. (Believe it or not, some bottled water is more expensive per gallon than gasoline). Look on the store shelves again and you will find that there are numerous brands of bottled water - all claiming to offer something different than the next brand.

Some claim to be more pure than other brands. Some claim to have fewer chemicals, some more minerals, and some claim to come from regions of the world where the environment is not as polluted as others. Still there's one fundamental claim that all of these brands of bottled water stick to. It's that they can quench your thirst.

We reflect upon this matter of being thirsty today because in this day and age, we thirst for many things. Some of us have schedules that are so full that they leave us thirsty for time with God.   Some of us have religion in our lives, and yet our relationship with the Lord yearns for intimacy.

Some of us thirst for recognition from others as a way of masking our deeper need for self-esteem. Some of us thirst for relationships – only to find ourselves being exploited and abused and unable to deal with our profound loneliness. We thirst for material things and find ourselves mired in a form of "affluenza", which Marion Wright Edelman of the Children's Defense Fund has defined as our "possessing too much that is worth too little". We thirst.

What are you thirsty for? What are the things that you most desire in life? What are your heart's desires? What are the things that you seek after?

Over the course of history, there have been persons who have thirsted for the things that would make our world better, the things of God:

- Martin Luther King, Jr. thirsted for racial equality.
- Mohandas Gandhi thirsted for peace and justice.
- Mother Theresa thirsted for truth and fairness.
- Dietrich Bonheoffer thirsted for true discipleship.
- Rosa Parks thirsted for her dignity.

We are reminded here of the story of the Samaritan Woman at the Well as depicted in the Gospel of John (John 4). At noon, the woman stopped by the well of Sycar to draw water. The disciples were in a nearby village getting bread, and Jesus was alone at the well as the woman approached. Jesus engaged this woman in conversation and asked her for a drink. When his disciples returned and saw Jesus talking to the woman, they were outraged. First, the woman was considered to be an untouchable for she was not a Jew. She was a Samaritan who represented some of the social outcasts of ancient Palestine. Second, social convention prohibited a first century man from speaking to a woman in public unless it was his wife. Third, this woman was considered to be defiled because she had been divorced five times, and was considered to be living in adultery.

This Samaritan woman came seeking to draw water. And there she met Jesus. She may have even come to the well possessing some sense of what it meant to be religious, but she had not encountered God on the level of intimacy which Jesus offered her. Jesus said to her, "I will give you living water – I will give you water that will not only satisfy your physical needs, but water that will satisfy your spiritual needs."

Jesus realized that what this woman really thirsted for – what she really needed - like many of us - was living water. What she really needed is what we all need - a relationship with the living water – Jesus Christ - the thirst-quencher.

What Jesus sought to convey to this woman and seeks to convey to you and me is that he is *the living water*. He is the life-giving water who will satisfy all of our needs. He will sustain and keep us. The living water that Jesus is, leaves us needing no other. He's the thirst-quencher.

Christ beckons each of us today to *obey our thirst*. This should be good news for us today. In the midst of failing economies, political disappointment, violence and wars, broken homes, dysfunctional families, lost jobs, unstable communities and diminished stock portfolios – Jesus is *the living water*. In the midst of doubts, dread, despair, distress, disillusionment, disappointment – Jesus is *the living water*.

For what are you thirsty, today? Are you thirsting after God? Many of us are like the psalmist, and can declare, *"My soul thirsts for God, for the living God."* I've simply come to suggest that the Lord desires that we obey our thirst, and seek after him – who is our thirst-quencher. Our response to the presence, provision and power of the living God should be to obey our thirst, and seek the Lord where and while God can be found.

I have decided to follow Jesus…
No turning back, no turning back.
The world behind me, the cross before me…
No turning back, no turning back.

Chapter 6
BETTER TOGETHER

How very good and pleasant it is when kindred live together in unity! It is like precious oil on the head, running down upon the beard, on the beard of Aaron, running down over the collar of his robes. It is like the dew of Hermon, which fall on the mountains of Zion. For there the Lord ordained his blessing, life forevermore. (Psalm 133:1-3)

A careful reading of scripture points with clarity to God's divine design for all of humanity. The assertion that God has created all of humanity in God's image was first recorded in the Bible in the Book of Genesis and reminds us that God's purpose for us is rooted in our God-likeness. And it is in our God-likeness that we find our commonality in Christ.

Because of our God-likeness, the fact of the matter is we are more alike than we are different. In-fact, the Human Genome Project reports that DNA of different humans is greater than ninety-nine percent alike, with only a few letters out of three billion in each of our DNA code changing our physical appearance. There is very little that is really different about us. We are far more similar than we are different.

One challenge for us in the present age is that we tend to focus more on the things that are different among us, than on our similarities. This challenge is exacerbated by the fact that the focus and fixation on our differences tends to lead to divisions within the human family.

History is littered with horrific examples of humans unable to live in love and harmony with others. As we look around, it is easy to see that we are separated in many ways. Segregation, discrimination and disintegration continue to be pervasive among us. Indeed, our churches and our society in general continue to deal with the problems of racism, sexism, and elitism. We see separation in the forms of denominationalism and traditionalism extant in many churches. We see it in ongoing political division and social alienation.

It is my belief that such separation leads to a form of human isolation that places too many of us outside the divine order and intent of God. Such separation forces us to go in one of two directions. First, many of us find ourselves wanting to go it alone, and live life outside of community altogether. This is what might be called the "me-my-and-I" syndrome, where we turn inward and focus mainly, if not exclusively, on ourselves and how we will succeed in life. Here, our lives are privatized in ways that stunt our growth as social beings, and we turn more and more inward for meaning in life, and seek less and less to share life with our sisters and brothers.

Or second, we go down the road of simply seeking to share in community only with persons who are the most like us. This is the "birds of a feather" syndrome, where we find ourselves flocking together with persons who look like us, talk like us, think like us, believe like us, sing like we sing, pray like we pray, go to the same places that we go, and do the same things that we do.

In either case, we are like caterpillars that never leave the cocoon - stuck inside our own selves – trapped within our own possibilities, lost in the midst of life itself, never able to fully realize what and who we are to become.

How might we overcome these tendencies toward isolation and segregation? In Psalm 133, the psalmist offers encouragement and hope as to how we might better live our lives together. The psalmist declares in the opening words here, *"How very good and pleasant it is for sisters and brothers to dwell together in unity!"*

The main theme of the psalm is the reunification of the northern and southern kingdoms of Israel. The psalmist here uses family imagery to evoke the joy and blessedness of living together in unity. This psalm speaks to the church and the whole family of God, and reminds us of God's ideal that we break down barriers and walls of division, and join with those who have been estranged from fellowship with God and God's church. These are words of faith and life for those seeking true community. The psalmist points to the blessing that is found for those of us who are a part of the family of God being able to dwell together in unity.

The thing that is important to first notice is that the psalmist points to the blessing of not simply dwelling together, but *dwelling together in unity*. Certainly, the psalmist might have stopped by saying that it is blessed that we dwell together, but he shared that it's very good and pleasant when we *dwell together in unity*.

In community, we seek to arrive at a relationship with others where we are not necessarily one, but where we dwell together in unity (Psalm 133:1), cognizant always of the realistic balance between being self-concerned and being other-concerned.

Desmond Tutu, in his nonviolent battle against apartheid in South Africa, rallied around the concept of *Ubuntu*, "I am what I am because of who we all are, and therefore, because of who we are, I am." *Ubuntu* speaks to the very quality of being human, affirms the fundamental humanness of us all, and asserts the support that we must afford each other if we are to be all that God calls us to be. Ultimately, the work of Tutu and those who worked with him - centered in *Ubuntu* - turned the tide on South African apartheid and opened the way for peace, equality, justice and forgiveness.

The psalmist here points to unity as a goal that we must achieve if we are to be whole. It is a vision that we must be committed to living.

My grandmother made vegetable soup the way I think the Holy Spirit can bring about unity among us, and in a way that I think speaks to the psalmist's intend in Psalm 133. She would imagine what needed to go into the pot to make the soup taste just right. She would add the right vegetables, meat and seasoning to the pot, in the right order, at just the right time, and cook it at the right temperature, for the exact amount of time - so that when it was done, the soup was cooked to near perfection.

In a similar way, God can take who we are – as different as we all are from each other – and enable us not to just live together, but to live together in ways that make our witness nourishment for each other and the world. God's power in the world rests, in large measure, in our unity. *We're better together.*

Indeed, we find strength in dwelling together in unity. God created us to be in community, and community makes us stronger. There's an African proverb that says, "A finger can't pick up a grain, it takes a whole hand." The strength of our lives - the strength of the church and our community - depends not on a finger, but on the whole hand.

In ancient Greek literature there is a story that shows the power of working together, or synergism.

"An aged, dying father called his seven sons around him. He gave each one a stick and told them to break it. Each son easily broke his separate stick. The old father then bound seven sticks together, and gave the bundle to his eldest son and told him to break the bundle. The eldest son could not break it. Then the second son was commanded to try. He could not break it, nor could any of the rest.

"So is it to be of you," said the father. Alone you are weak, but together you are strong."

Synergism is derived from the Greek word "*synergos*" meaning "working together." It means that by joining with others, common objectives can be more easily and effectively accomplished. There is strength in numbers when we multiply our efforts through living and working with others. *We're better together.*

The apostle Paul used the image of the body to make this point. One body part is not sufficient for life. It takes all of the body parts working together to make the body work as it should. So it is with the Body of Christ – the church. *We're better together.* Maybe it was the case that the Israelites in the days when the psalmist penned this song were a lot like we are today. Maybe they needed to know, as we need to know today, that *we're better together.*

In his popular song, Hezekiah Walker shares words that remind us of the very things that our lives depend on today:
I need you, you need me.
We're all a part of God's body.
Stand with me, agree with me.
We're all a part of God's body.
It is God's will that every need be supplied.
You are important to me, I need you to survive.

I pray for you, you pray for me.
We're all a part of God's body.
I won't harm you with words from my mouth.
I love you. I need you to survive.

I simply came to remind us that *we're better together*!

Chapter 7
A REASON TO CELEBRATE

If it had not been for the Lord who was on our side – let Israel now say – if it had not been for the Lord who was on our side, when our enemies attacked us, then they would have swallowed us up alive, when their anger was kindled against us; then the flood would have swept us away, the torrent would have gone over us; then over us would have gone the raging waters. (Psalm 124:1-5)

I believe that most – if not all - of us would agree that these are days filled with many ups and downs. It seems more than ever that life is like a roller coaster. From the collapse of the economy that has affected all of us – to the wars that are now being fought in at least three places in the Middle East – to the election of the first African American to the highest office in the land – recent days have been filled with what one song-writer called "swift transition".

Indeed, these images are etched in our memories across virtually every sector of society today. We saw signs of joy and celebration on election night – when at about 11:00 pm on November 4, 2008 – celebrations began among many people across the land with the election of Barack Obama as the 44th president of the United States.

I don't believe I was alone where when the election results came in from California, I picked up the telephone and called just about everybody I could think of to celebrate that moment of history. Still etched in our collective memory is the crowd of over

100,000 people who gathered in the night at Grant Park in Chicago to celebrate Barack Obama's election. Less than three weeks ago on January 20, 2009, Washington, DC was filled with people sharing in the celebration of the inauguration of President Obama.

And just a few days ago, people all over the world gathered in front of television sets to watch the Super Bowl. Whether you were rooting for the Pittsburgh Steelers or the Arizona Cardinals, there were moments of cheering and celebration for many of us throughout the course of the game.

Each of these occasions – and others - leads us to reflect upon the very nature of celebration in our contemporary culture. One of the most critical components of celebration is the (usual) insinuation of a celebrity – somebody (or at the least something) worthy of being celebrated. When we attend a birthday party, or a bridal reception, or a retirement banquet, or even a New Year's Eve party, we are going because somebody or something is being celebrated.

There's a reason to celebrate. In our contemporary culture we find that celebrity has become a rather fleeting concept. Too often, we confer the term "celebrity" on persons who have barely accomplished anything in life. A rap artist or singer who may have one or two hit recordings is considered to be a celebrity. A movie actor or actress with one or two outstanding films to his or her credit is considered to be a celebrity. A reality television show star becomes an instant celebrity. And an athlete with one or two successful seasons meets with instant notoriety, and overnight is considered to be a celebrity.

These apparent reasons to celebrate indeed are often fleeting – here today and often forgotten tomorrow. But I want to suggest to us that there is a reason to celebrate that doesn't have anything to do with the highs and lows of the economy, the cost of gasoline, bailouts of banks and other businesses, or even who the next president will be. This reason to celebrate has nothing to do with who the biggest box office hit is, or who has the latest hit recording, or who has the biggest sports contract, or the most YouTube hits, or the most popular TED Talk, or the most Facebook friends.

There is a reason to celebrate that is more profound and important than all of these. This is what David was trying to help us understand in Psalm 124. David asked the question, *"If it had not been for the Lord who was on our side... where would we be?"*

David was trying to remind the Israelites of all that they had gone through.   But he didn't want them to stop with remembering what they had gone through – he wanted to also let them know who it was that had brought them through.   Yes, they had gone through some things, but he wanted them to remember who had brought them out.

The Israelites needed to remember that God had made a way for them - God had been with them through all of their ups and downs -

- At the Red Sea - God had been with them and delivered them from Egyptian bondage.
- At the Jordan River - God had been with them, and made a way for them to get to the Promised Land.
- Through many dangers, through many toils, and through many snares - God had been with them.

And now they had a reason to celebrate with a victory song and to declare how God had brought them through - *"If it had not been for the Lord who was on our side..."*

If you know like I know, many of us are like David and the Israelites. We can look back over our lives, and we can declare that *"If it had not been for the Lord who was on our side..."* All of us have gone through some things that have brought us to this point in our lives. We've gone through some points of disappointment and discouragement, some trials and tribulations. And if we take a moment to look back and recollect, we realize that it was the Lord who brought us through. Indeed, we have *a reason to celebrate.*

One contemporary song-writer helps us to see that David's words are for us. Marvin Sapp sings:

I never would have made it,
I never could have made it
Without you;
I would have lost it all
But I now see how you were there for me…

Yes, maybe David knew that we would need this assurance for the living of the days that are ours. Maybe David knew that at some point, some persons of faith – regardless of how faithful you are – would still be facing sickness in your body…death of a loved one…an eviction notice…a pink slip on your job…more month than money.

Indeed, there are those among us who may sense that there is no reason to celebrate. The poor, the hungry and the homeless are still among us. Many children awaken each day with no food to eat. Many people have been gripped by addiction. Many families have been affected by violence and death.

And yet, as people of faith and hope, we know that in the midst of it all, there is still a reason to celebrate. And when we know that we have a reason to celebrate, we'll have a testimony.

The song-writer said it best when it was penned, "When I look back over my life, and think things over, I can truly say, that

I've been blessed, I've got a testimony."

David had a testimony, and he beckoned the people of Israel to share their testimony. I've come to understand that those who really have a testimony can give a first-hand account of something they've seen, heard or experienced in their life. One who has a testimony has been a witness to the goodness of the Lord.

Think about a court case. One who is asked to testify in a court case has a first-hand account of something they've seen, heard or experienced, and thus they are in a position to offer a testimony to the judge and jury. We likewise can and should have a testimony when we've seen, heard or experienced the prevenience, provision and power of God in our lives. And our testimony should give us reason not only to tell of what God has done, but a reason to celebrate what God is doing, and is about to do in our lives.

David gave a testimony to Israel through his question. *"If it had not been for the Lord who was on our side... where would we be?"* Marvin Sapp gave a testimony in his song – "I'm stronger, better and wiser" with the Lord in my life.

My testimony is that "When I think of the goodness of Jesus, and all that God has done for me, my soul cries out "hallelujah"; I thank God for saving me!"

We have a reason to celebrate!
- God brought us out … without a doubt. We can celebrate!
- God saved us… and raised us. We can celebrate!
- God made a way out of no way. We can celebrate!
- God has been good all the time … and all the time, God has been good!

We've got a reason to celebrate!

Section Two
Songs of Comfort
and Encouragement

Chapter 8
THROUGH...

Yea though I walk through the valley of the shadow of death, I will fear no evil, for thou art with me. (Psalm 23:4)

Like many of you, and many Christians around the world, I have found Psalm 23 to be a living scripture. It is not unusual for Christians to be able to recite this particular text. In many ways, Psalm 23 has become the primary text for many of our lives – the theme song for many of us who live in the Judeo-Christian faith traditions.

David's words, in many ways, have become our words – words that speak to the depth and breadth of the human condition. For those who are lonely, these words serve as a comfort and companion. For the hurting, there's healing. For those in despair, these are hopeful words.

Indeed, these are life-giving words. And every time I read the 23rd Psalm or hear these words recited, something different seems to touch me. In reading through the text most recently, that which came in and took residence with me was the word "through."

In the middle of this poetic text – this song of praise that David is singing here - he shares these memorable words:

*"Yea though I walk **through** the valley of the shadow of death, I will fear no evil, for thou art with me. Thy rod and thy staff, they comfort me."*

If you know like I know, many of us have no problem relating to what David is saying here. What David is speaking of when he says, *"Yea though I walk through…"* is what philosopher Cornel West has spoken of in terms of a certain nihilism that has taken residence in much of our life today. Indeed, as West suggests, a certain nihilism - a lovelessness, meaninglessness, and emptiness – an apparent hopelessness - seems to have pervaded our culture and permeated much of our reality.

This nihilism is clearly evident in the fact that we have more African-American males in prison than in college today. There are more black men in prison today than there were in slavery in America in 1859. Black and Hispanic males are imprisoned at over 6 times the rate of others in our country. This is what Michelle Alexander, in her book, calls "The New Jim Crow," where the disproportionate incarceration of black and brown men – who have become convicted felons – has effectively created a permanent underclass of men whose rights are restricted in America when they are released from prison, and who therefore often can't vote, have very limited access to educational opportunities that would help them become self-sufficient, productive citizens, and who have extreme difficulty finding decent employment.

This nihilism is also seen in the fact that unemployment and underemployment is rampant in our nation… it is witnessed in the fact that addiction and death ravages many of our city streets (in Baltimore there were nearly 200 murders in 2011and over 340 in 2015, and the majority of these were of young African-American men under the age of thirty). The tragedy of this nihilism is that too much of our reality - in too many of our communities - is perpetually mired in depression and in despair.

And here in the 23rd Psalm, this nihilism – the very real ways that people are going through - is what David is trying to help us come to grips with. David described his own going through as a valley experience. In fact it was not just any valley - David called it the *"valley of the shadow of death."*

Eugene Peterson in *The Message* translation of the text calls the valley that David spoke of "Death Valley." It was a valley filled with darkness, death and despair – with no hope and no joy.

We don't know exactly what valley David was referring to here, but we do know he was talking about having gone through something:

- Maybe the valley that David is talking about was the attempts that King Saul had made to take David's life.
- Maybe is it was David's adulterous affair with Bathsheba.
- Maybe it was David's murder of Bathsheba's husband Uriah.

We don't know exactly what it was, but we do know that David was talking about having gone through a very real soul-torturing valley experience in his life.

Many of us can relate on a personal level to whatever David was going through:

- Going through what Job declared as "days filled with trouble."
- Going through what John of the Cross called "the dark night of the soul."
- Going through what black Mississippi sharecropper and political activist Fannie Lou Hamer described as being "sick and tired of being sick and tired."

- Going through what the singer of the hymn said was "sometimes feeling like a motherless child – a long way from home."
- Going through sleepless nights and darkened days.

Indeed, most of us can relate to going through. And if you are finding it difficult to relate, just live a little and you will experience from time to time:

- Sickness in your family
- Death at your doorstep
- A pink slip on your desk
- Difficulty making it from paycheck to paycheck (more month than money)
- Marital or relationship problems
- Problems with your children
- Times when our children and women may go through abuse and neglect.

Everybody will go through something at some point. And David was talking about the very real predicament of going through. And if you know like I know, when you are going through, it can become easy to feel that you are "too through," and want to give up and throw in the towel.

But lest we get stuck on David's (or our) predicament of going through, let me remind us that it's good that David did not stop with the fact that he had gone through or was going through something. In the midst of his going through, he didn't stop his song there - he kept singing:

"I will fear no evil. For (Lord) you are with me. Your rod and staff comfort me."

David kept singing because he knew that God would not bring him *to* anything that God would not take him *through*. This ought to be good news to somebody who has come to a crossroads in your life. If you are a person of faith, you can keep singing because you know that whatever God has brought you to, God will take you through.

And there's even more good news in knowing that if you are going through, it means that you are not stuck.

And you can rejoice in knowing that your going through – your testing and trial - is really a precursor to your testimony… and that at the end of your coming to the difficult situations of life, and your going through these situations, God is really preparing your life for a *breakthrough*.

The Apostle Paul talked about going through in Romans 8 when he declared that *"the suffering of this present day is not worthy to be compared to the glory that shall be revealed in us."* (v.18) And later in that chapter, Paul said that *"all things work together for the good of those who love the Lord and are called according to his purpose."* (v.28) Like David, Paul wanted to remind us that God can get some glory even out of our going through.

And finally, we see in Psalm 23 that when God brings us through, we ought to keep singing. David continued his song not by talking about having gone through, but by talking about the presence and provision of the Lord.

He said, *"(Lord) you prepare a table for me in the presence of my enemies. My cup runs over."*

It's good to know that on the other side of going through, God will provide all that we need, when we need it. And therefore, David could end his signature psalm with a praise offering to God. He ended with a **doxology** - an act of praise to his God.

"Surely, goodness and mercy will follow me all the days of my life, and I will dwell in the house of the Lord forever."

We may be going through, but thank God, we're not going through alone.   We may be going through, but it's good to know that we have God's grace and mercy to bring us through. We may be going through, but we know that with God, we're coming out!

Chapter 9
WAIT ON THE LORD

I believe that I shall see the goodness of the Lord in the land of the living. Wait for the Lord; be strong, and let your heart take courage; wait for the Lord! (Psalm 27:13-14)

(This sermon was first preached in 2002 on the brink of the United States government's decision to go to war with Iraq.)

In a phenomenal little book entitled *Addicted to Hurry*, Dr. Kirk Byron Jones addresses a matter that is endemic and epidemic in our contemporary culture. Jones reminds us of our conspicuous propensity towards rushing. We are addicted to hurry. Indeed, hurry is one of the marks of our society.

It is very apparent that too many people are in too much of a hurry, to accomplish too many things, and see too many people, and go to too many places. We are mired in a compulsive obsession with speed.

Yes, we are a world that is in a hurry. We're in a hurry to get to work, a hurry to get to school, a hurry to get to church, and a hurry to get to the store.

We're in a hurry. We're in a hurry to vacation, and in a hurry to retire. We're in a hurry to order our food, a hurry to eat our food, and in a hurry to pay for our food. We're in a hurry to matriculate, a hurry to graduate, a hurry to marry, and some are even in a hurry to get divorced.

We're in a hurry for medical care, a hurry for lawyer's advice, a hurry to lose weight, and in a hurry to look good. We're in a hurry to make money, a hurry to spend money, and some of us may even be in a hurry to save some money. We're in a hurry to buy the car, a hurry to buy the house, and a hurry to buy the wide-screen or flat-screen television set (with remote control).

We want all that life has to offer – and we want it quick, fast and in a hurry!

It seems that now we, as a nation, are even in a hurry to go to war. We seem to be in a hurry to inflict bloodshed, and in a hurry to bomb the homes, and schools, and mosques of persons in far off lands.

So often it seems that in the midst of our rush to get things done, and to go from place to place, we fail to see what is really going on around us. As a parent, I must confess that I am often amazed when I take time to actually observe my children, and how they are maturing.

I can see them every day, live with them, eat with them, and take them to their various activities, but I must confess that I am often in so much of a hurry to perform these "acts" of fatherhood, that I don't take the quality time to actually see what is really going on in their lives - to savor and relish how they're growing and changing and maturing.

I'm reminded of a book that comedian Bill Cosby wrote several years ago entitled, *Time Flies*. Often in the midst of our hurriedness and rushing, time is flying by so fast that we don't really see what is occurring before our very eyes.

Indeed, it is the case that our hurriedness has become more pronounced and exacerbated. Time is flying. Endemic to our societal reality is that people are apt to push to the front of the line, cars speed ahead, and we are all left to wonder whether we will ever be able to slow down.

And amidst our hurriedness, it seems that we have lost a sense of connectedness and community – a sense of common interest and genuine concern for one another. It seems that we've lost much of our capacity to pause and wait - and savor and relish the meaning of life and our common plight as the people of God.

It seems that the psalmist here in the 27th Psalm had a concern similar to the dilemmas facing us contemporarily. He declares to those to whom he is writing that they are to *"wait on the Lord, be strong, and be of good courage."*

It is obvious here that those in the faith community had not yet learned or had forgotten how to wait on the Lord. It's plain to see that they needed a reminder of the importance of not depending solely on their own resources and recourses. It is clear that they had forgotten that God acts in God's time, and what they really needed to do was wait on God, and that eventually God would show up in their lives. They needed to wait.

Likewise, we are beckoned to stop… take a deep breath… and wait on the Lord.

But let us not get too comfortable in our waiting. For as soon as some folk hear that we need to wait on God, our minds wander into a state of *do-nothing-ness*, where somehow we think we can sit around and wait on the Lord to do everything for us. But this is not what the psalmist meant when he said wait on the Lord.

What exactly, then, does this waiting entail?

In the psalmist's encouragement and admonition to wait on the Lord – I believe there are three lessons that we can learn - three things that waiting on the Lord entails.

First, *waiting involves watching.* The psalmist was encouraging people of faith to watch and observe the signs of how God was about to appear in their lives. For faithful people, waiting always entails *watching and praying.* We wait, but we wait and watch with expectancy that God is going to show us a better way. In these difficult and distressing days, what signs do we see as to the presence of the Lord in our world?

Second, to wait on the Lord means that *we will be involved in working.* The psalmist's words that people of faith were to wait had a subsequent line that they were to be of good courage. They were to take courage – and they were to work while they waited on the Lord. It takes courage to get up in the midst of our waiting, and to work while we wait. It takes courage to prepare ourselves spiritually for what God has in store for us. It takes courage to persist and persevere in the midst of waiting. What are we doing to prepare ourselves spiritually, relationally, emotionally, intellectually, and physically for the blessings that God has in store for us?

Third, waiting on the Lord also involves *worshipping.* We are reminded that all that was written in the Psalms was written within the context of worship. The psalmist said, *"Wait on the Lord, be strong, and let your hearts take courage."* This meant that as the Israelites waited, they needed to keep worshipping God. As they waited, they needed to praise God because of God's steadfast love and provision in their lives. How have we determined to worship the One who is our Reason... the one who created us….the one who saved us… the one who keeps us?

Wait on the Lord!

It has been said that waiting is the highest order of discipline. I don't know about you - but I believe that given the condition of our world, we need to learn how wait on the Lord more than ever before.

What happens when we wait on the Lord?

- When we wait on the Lord, we realize that love and grace are more powerful than all of the negativity and destruction incumbent in our world today.
- When we wait on the Lord, we realize that hope is possible amidst hostility… destiny amidst devastation and despair… possibility amidst pestilence… and victory amidst virulence.

Wait on the Lord!

I know that it might not always be easy to wait, but I'm glad to tell you that some folk came along before us to teach us how to wait.

- The children of Israel waited on the Lord in the wilderness for 40 years.
- Job in his trouble said I'm going to wait on the Lord until my change comes.
- And Isaiah came along and gave us a song to remind us what happens when we wait on the Lord. Isaiah preached:

Even youths grow weary and faint
But, they that wait on the Lord
Will renew their strength
They will mount up with wings as eagles
They will run and not be weary
They will walk and not faint! (Isa. 40:31)

When we wait on the Lord -
Every valley will be exalted
Every hill and every mountain will be made low
The uneven ground shall become level
And the rough places made plain.

And the glory of the Lord shall be revealed,
And all people shall see it
For in Jesus (the Lord of Lords, and the King of Kings)
God has shown up!

Chapter 10
THE COMPANY-KEEPER

I have been young, and now am old; yet I have not seen the righteous forsaken or their children begging for bread. (Psalm 37:25)

As we look around and consider life and living in this present day – we realize that there are tremendous amounts of loneliness, isolation and separation in our world today.

For the great 20th century theologian Paul Tillich, humanity's existential estrangement from God is essentially sin. I would take Tillich's argument a step further to suggest that humanity's estrangement from humanity – our estrangement from one another – is also sin.

Those beliefs, attitudes, and behaviors that serve to separate us – and segregate us – and alienate us – and estrange us – are sinful and antithetical to the desires and ways of God. It is God's desire – God's will - to draw us near to the divine – and near to one another.

That is why the psalmist reminded the community of faith that it was *"very good and pleasant for sisters and brothers to live in unity."* (Psalm 133:1)

What we realize is that to live in shalom – in unity – in community – and on a deeper level - in communion – is a blessing from God. This is God's desire for us. God does not will for us – God does not desire for us - to be estranged, separated, alienated or segregated from each other. It is when the "isms' and "schisms" of life are the most present that we find ourselves in an experience – an existence – a reality – that is outside of God's will for us.

Whether this separation manifests itself in forms of racism, or sexism, or classism, or materialism, or militarism, or elitism, or intellectualism, or denominationalism - we find ourselves living outside the will of God.

Whether separation is found in the many distorted forms of fundamentalism, or liberalism, or nationalism, or tribalism – we find ourselves living outside the will of God.

Whatever the "ism" or "schism" – if it serves to alienate us from God, and separate us from each other, then it is sinful.

In Psalm 37, we find that the psalmist offers us words of assurance and hope amidst the alienation and separation of this world. We are encouraged with these words:

"Do not fret because of the wicked; do not be envious of wrongdoers, for they will fade away like the grass."

The psalmist later declares in his affirmation of faith in God, that:
"I've been young and now am old, but I've never seen the righteous forsaken, or their children begging for bread."

Why is the psalmist led here to deal with this matter of forsakenness? Obviously, the psalmist, as he had grown older, had lived through some things, and he could now attest to the fact that experience is often the best teacher. He and those to whom he spoke had gone through this condition of forsakenness – being separated from God, and from one another. And so, he knew what it was like to be lonely. He knew what it was like to travel up the rough side of the mountain – alone. He knew what it was like to need a friend, but to find it difficult to find one.

But now as the psalmist looks back over his life, he can declare:

"I've never seen the righteous forsaken – or their children begging for bread."

We need to be reminded of these words today because we will all be where the psalmist found himself. Certainly, sometimes the people we thought we could trust and count on the most will forsake us. Sometimes the most certain - and apparently most promising of circumstances and conditions will lead to disappointment, discouragement and even depression.

We are reminded daily that disappointments are inevitable. Trials and tribulations really will show up if we live long enough. Temptations will meet and greet each of us. Somebody said that "every tub has its bottom." And sometimes – if you know like I know - we will find ourselves at that bottom.

And we in the church – we the people of faith - need to realize that we are not immune to the trials of life. Trials will come to meet and greet even the most faithful among us. Sometimes it seems that the more faithful we are, the more trials that will come our way.

We try praying through our troubles. We try singing through them. We try preaching our way out. But we find no refuge.

We go to counselors and psychologists. We read every self-help book and attend every self-help session we can find. We watch Oprah Winfrey and Dr. Phil (McGraw), but we can't seem to find our way out.

We need to remember that even Jesus found himself at the point of feeling forsaken. Jesus found himself hanging on a cross, betrayed and let down and denied even by some of those who had been the closest to him, dying with no help to be found. Jesus was feeling forsaken, and all the Lord could do was cry out, *"My God, my God why have you forsaken me."* (Matthew 27:46)

This is what the psalmist was trying to remind us of. All of us will find ourselves at this place at some point. But what the psalmist was also trying to tell you and me is that regardless of how bad things might appear - as difficult as things might seem - we are never really forsaken by God. God will not forsake us or foreclose on us. God is a company-keeper for you and for me.

The question then is, "how do we reach the point in our lives where we can live with this assurance that God is our company-keeper?"

The psalmist points us to three things that we need to do on our faith journey, as we walk along this inevitable and arduous path of loneliness and despair in order to realize this assurance of God's presence.

First, we need to *trust in the Lord*. The writer of Proverbs affirmed our need to trust God. He said, *"Trust in the Lord with all thy heart and lean not to thy own understanding. In all your ways acknowledge God, and God will direct your path."* (Proverbs 3:5-6) Trust means living with the assurance that God will come through for us because of what we know that God has already done in our lives. We trust God because God is trustworthy.

Second, we need to *take delight in the Lord*. Sometimes we need to keep praising our way through our situation. To take delight in the Lord is to revel in God's goodness, and know that the Lord is delightful in all God's ways.

Third, we need to *commit our ways to the Lord*. When we commit our ways to the Lord, we are engaging in the process hanging in there. When we commit our ways to the Lord, we are engaging in the process of holding onto God's unchanging hand –

because we know that our help is on the way. For we know that as we hang in there – as we hold on - as we begin to let the Lord work on our behalf, real change begins to occur in our lives.

When we can **trust** God, and **delight** in the Lord (even in our trials), and **commit** our ways to God's ways, then we are able to surrender to the Lord.

It is at the point of our surrender that we learn how to wait on the Lord and we begin to find strength and hope in God. The song-writer said that:

"(Jesus is) our help in ages pasts, our hope for days to come, a shelter in times of storm, and our eternal home."

I'm glad that Jesus promised us that "I'll never leave you or forsake you."   And we can rest assured that he's our company-keeper.

- Trouble at home – He's a company-keeper.
- Trouble on your job – He's a company-keeper.
- Trouble at school – He's a company-keeper.
- Trouble at church – He's a company-keeper.
- Trouble with your finances… sickness in your body… trouble with friends… trouble with enemies … He's a company-keeper.

I've come to remind us that the Lord is a company-keeper.

The song-writer said it best:
There's not a friend like the lowly Jesus
No not one, no not one…

And another song-writer said it just as well:

> I've seen the lightening flashing
> And I've heard the thunder roll,
> I've felt sin's breakers dashing
> Trying to conquer my soul,
> I heard the voice of my Jesus
> Telling me still to fight on,
> He promised
> Never to leave me
> Never to leave me alone!

Chapter 11
WORDS TO THE WISE

Fools say in their hearts, "There is no God." They are corrupt, they commit abominable acts; God looks down from heaven on humankind to see if there are any who are wise, who seek after God. (Psalm 53:1-2)

It is very apparent that we live in times of tremendous skepticism and unbelief. These are times when it is difficult to place one's faith and trust in anything or anybody. Politicians and business leaders have too often been caught in corruption and immorality – placing a pall upon our view of many of those who choose to engage in political and corporate life.

Many persons in vocations and professions that have traditionally been considered "helping" professions have also now been found to have engaged in activities and behaviors that betray the trust of those who have placed their trust in these persons.

Indeed, even doctors, teachers and ministers, those who have typically been viewed as being among the most trustworthy among us, are now often viewed with eyes of skepticism, cynicism and distrust.

This causes a dilemma for persons of faith – particularly when church leaders are found to be among the untrustworthy and fallen among us. Over time - for many persons of faith - pastors, priests, rabbis and imams have represented the very face of God. The words and actions of religious leaders have been viewed by many among the faithful as the words and actions of God.

And so when religious leaders fall, fail and disappoint – people's belief, faith and trust in God may often be challenged, and their faith might begin to fracture and shatter, if not break all together. The extreme reality in this possible breaking of faith is what philosopher Freidrich Nietzsche, among others, would characterize to as the "death of God." These are moments when our faith is challenged – and our notion of the presence – the reality of God – is brought into question in a serious way.

Our sense of the presence of God - as moral reality and absolute truth - diminishes with the immorality, corruption, sinfulness and brokenness of those persons who are deemed to be those called to represent the face of God.

And so the quest begins for an answer. In what and in whom might we place our trust and belief today? How do we keep trusting and believing in God amidst all the fallenness that is incumbent among us?

In Psalm 53:1-2, we find words to the wise. Here it is declared that *"only fools do not trust and believe God. But the wise trust in and seek after the Lord."* It appears that the psalmist was dealing with some people who had been living in a state of distrust of and disbelief in God. They had turned their backs on God, and turned their lives away from God. The psalmist declares that *"only fools say there is no God."*

And if we look around us, we realize that the world really hasn't changed much since the days of the psalmist. Today, we find that too many people have placed their trust in too many people and things that are outside the will of God.

Contemporary thinking might lead us to place our trust and belief in so many realities that are not God and things that are not of God. How many of us lately have found ourselves placing our trust and belief in something or somebody only to find out that our trust and belief were misguided? Somebody has promised us something only to disappoint us. We're promised love and affection, a promotion on our jobs, or certain recognition - and we find ourselves disappointed because our expectations are unfulfilled.

The psalmist goes on to point out, *"the wise trust in the Lord."* Those of us who would be wise today – those who would be filled with wisdom – would learn to place our trust and faith in God.

These are words to the wise. To trust and believe in God is to know that beyond the realm of our humanity, and our bent toward those people and things that might disappoint us, God never disappoints. To trust and believe in God – to know God - is to be wise. That is why it is written in scripture that *"knowledge of the Lord is the beginning of wisdom."*

Now we can see why those of past generations seemed to have a wisdom that so many people today don't possess - because they trusted in the Lord. There was no Internet and no information age, but they trusted in the Lord. The world was not always at their finger-tips - there were no cell phones, no laptop computers or IPads. There was not cable television, but they trusted in the Lord.

Often their ministers were not well educated, many did not have the benefit of a college or even a high school education, but they trusted in the Lord. *Knowledge of the Lord is the beginning of wisdom.* A word to the wise today is that we need to get re-acquainted and reconnected with Jesus.

What happens when we get to know the Lord?

- When we get to know the Lord, God improves our *attitude*. God begins to change our behaviors and the ways that we act toward God and each other.

- When we get to know the Lord, God improves our *aptitude*. God begins to change our minds and the way we think about God, people and the world in general.
- When we get to know the Lord, God enhances our *altitude*. As we get to know the Lord, and live according to God's will for us, God begins to take us to new levels and higher heights in our endeavors.

That's what the song-write meant when it was written:
I'm pressing on the upward way
New heights I'm gaining every day
Still pressing on another round
Lord plant my feet on higher ground.

Chapter 12
A PLEA FOR HELP

Lord, have mercy on me according to your loving-kindness; according to your abundant mercy blot out my transgressions. (Psalm 51:1)

As we look around, we realize that we need the Lord more than ever before. If the truth is told, we're morally bankrupt as a society - it seems that virtually anything goes – if it feels good, do it. We find that political and corporate corruption abounds – and too many people are drunk with the prospects of wealth and power.

If we've ever needed the Lord before, we need God now. Many families are broken – children telling their parents what to do … and parents afraid to discipline and parent their children. We find death and destruction on our streets. I'm persuaded that we have a pervasive and abiding need for the Lord today.

I believe that the song of the great singer Marvin Gaye speaks to the conditions of our world today, and our need for help:

Oh, mercy mercy me
Oh, things ain't what they used to be
No, no
Where did all the blue sky go?
Poison is the wind that blows
From the north, east, south, and sea
Oh, mercy mercy me
Oh, things ain't what they used to be.

Given all that is occurring around us, I believe these are days when God is calling each of us to examine our lives and see where we might change – and where we might seek redirection on our life journeys.

It was St. Augustine who may have best captured this yearning when he prayed, "Lord you have created us for yourself, and our souls are restless until they find their rest in thee."

Indeed, in each of our lives, God has a way of getting our attention and letting us know of God's desire that we change direction. We find evidence of this in the scripture today. Many of us are familiar with the story.

Psalm 51 offers a depiction of a season in the life of David. Here, the psalmist cries out to God with a plea for mercy – a plea for help. Many scholars believe that this plea is in the aftermath of David's adulterous transgressions with Bathsheba, and the subsequent violent attack on Bathsheba's husband, Uriah.

And thus David's cry:
*"Lord, have mercy on me according to your lovingkindness…
according to your abundant mercy blot out my transgressions."*

Here, David was dealing with a need for help in his life. David lamented, he cried out because he found himself dealing with the very real problem of human weakness – fallenness and shortcomings in his life, and all he could do now was turn to God for help.

Careful reflection upon David's plea for help would indicate that he is not alone. Each of us has found ourselves at the place where we've needed God to step into our lives, and turn things around for us.

And lest we gloss over David's lament, let us remember

that he was not just crying to be crying. David was crying because he had a reason to cry. He was dealing with the existential reality of sin and spiritual separation from God. He had transgressed, he had gone against God's will; he had sinned and fallen short of the glory of God, and thus he needed mercy, he needed help.

And notice here that David does not speak in any particular way about his need - we just know that he is crying out for mercy. He does not name his burden - we just know that he's dealing with something in his life, and needs God's help.

Perhaps David realized that somebody else someday would benefit from his experience and knowing how he came through. Perhaps David knew that his personal place of sorrow and point of bitter tears was a place where we have all been…or will be … if we keep living.

Ultimately, we know that it is God's desire that we, like David, point our lives in the direction which God seeks for us to go. Like David, our journey is to be one of following the path that God has set out for us.

Redirection – changing directions is what God calls us to today. What are the areas in our lives, our homes, our churches, our communities and in our world where God is calling us to change directions? How have we gone in directions that are not pleasing to God?

One of the things we can know and love about the Lord is that God is a merciful God. When we are at our worst, God proves time and time again, that God is at God's best.

Mercy, I believe, stands as one of the most important and powerful aspects of our faith life – it is at the center of our walk with God. For you see, everybody at some point will need some mercy. Our need for mercy speaks to our sinfulness … our separation from God … our segregation and disintegration from the Lord – and thus our need for forgiveness and pardon by God.

Why do we need mercy? None of us can honestly declare that we meet all of God's standards of holiness and righteousness – all the time. None of us is perfect. As hard as we might try, we all come up short of God's expectations of us from time to time. As much as some of us might try to pretend that we never stray from God's ways, we all come up short, and thus our need for God's mercy.

Indeed, mercy implies our need for pardon – and our need to be pardoned implies that we are guilty of something. It is like the person who knows he has committed a crime, and now finds himself standing in court before a judge and jury. The verdict is handed down, and the criminal is pronounced to be "guilty as charged."

As the criminal faces his punishment for the crime he has committed – as he faces his sentence – the criminal might plead for mercy. If the judge is merciful, she or he might offer leniency – and act with compassion by granting a pardon. The criminal is still guilty of a crime, but because of the judge's mercy, the criminal doesn't receive the justice, the punishment he deserves.

We are still guilty of sinfulness – and yet God acts with mercy toward us.

In the spiritual, we hear of such a cry for mercy:
> O Lord have mercy…
> When I'm in trouble
> Have mercy Lord, have mercy Lord on me.

Another hymn said:
> I cried and I cried, I cried all night long
> I cried and I cried, until I found the Lord.
> I moaned and I moaned, I moaned all night long
> I moaned and I moaned, until I found the Lord.
> I just couldn't rest contented…
> Until I found the Lord.

And so what do we need to do to experience the mercy of God?

First, we need to comprehend *the mind of God.* We need to realize that God is a forgiving God, and that God's mind is merciful. That's why Isaiah could encourage the Israelites with words of hope in the midst of their waywardness. God said through Isaiah, *"I even I am he who will blot out your sins, and will not remember your sins."* (Isaiah 43:25)

God's mind is merciful. That's why the prophet Jeremiah would utter words of hope in the midst of his lament. Even as he cried over the plight of Israel, Jeremiah could declare that the *"steadfast love of the Lord never ceases, God's mercies never come to an end…"* (Lamentations 3:22-23) God's mind is merciful.

Second, we need to be in concert with the *move of God.* Once we know that God's mind is merciful, we can then get in step with the Lord, and experience the *move of God* in our lives. That is what David was really yearning for in Psalm 51 – the *move of God* in his life. David prayed to God: *"Create in me a clean heart, and renew in me the right spirit. Do not cast me away from your presence. And do not take your holy spirit from me."*

David wanted to be in God's presence, and he wanted the Lord to move in every aspect of his life.

That's why David could declare when he got his life back together that:

"Weeping may endure for a night, but joy comes in the morning." (Psalm 30:5)

God had moved on David's life. God had transformed him, and restored the joy of his salvation. We likewise need to be in touch and in tune with the move of God.

Third, we need to submit to the *mysterious and miraculous power of God.* In order to really experience the mercy of God, we have to allow the mysterious and miraculous power of God to take control of our lives.

I've simply come to remind us that this mysterious and miraculous power is manifest for us in the person of Jesus Christ. Paul said it best – *"God demonstrated God's love toward us in that while we were yet sinners Christ died for us."* (Romans 5:8) This is a power, a love and a mercy that will turn your life around.

This is what David was really praying to God for – *a mysterious, miraculous power* - a mercy that would redirect him and turn his life around.

One of the prevalent changes in our society today has been the emergence of the GPS – the global positioning system. Many of us today have GPS systems in our cars as a replacement for maps and atlases which used to suffice in helping us to get from place to place. One of the features of the GPS comes into play when the driver has taken a wrong turn and is about to get lost. A voice emerges in the car and will indicate that "you have made a wrong turn, and the system will now need to re-calculate your route."

Could it be that you've gotten off course and that God desires to re-calculate your route, to redirect your life, and invite you back into relationship with Christ?

Could it be that we might declare like Charles Wesley:
> Long our imprisoned spirits lay,
> Fast bound in sin and nature's night;
> Thine eye diffused a quickening ray;
> We woke, the dungeon flamed with light;
> Our chains fell off, our hearts were free,
> We rose, went forth, and followed thee.
> Our chains fell off, our hearts were free,
> We rose, went forth, and followed thee.

Thanks be to God for mercy!
> I have decided to follow Jesus,
> No turning back, no turning back.
> The world behind me, the cross before me,
> No turning back, no turning back....

Chapter 13
GOD KNOWS

> ***O Lord, you have searched me and known me. You know when I sit down and when I rise up; you discern my thoughts from far away. You search out my path and my lying down, and are acquainted with all my ways. Even before a word is on my tongue, O Lord you know it completely. You hem me in behind and before, and lay your hand upon me. Such knowledge is too wonderful for me; it is so high that I cannot attain it. (Psalm 139:1-6)***

A critical question that lingers within the context of human prayer - our relationality and ongoing conversation with God – pertains to the nature of God's knowledge of the human predicament. What does God *really* know about who we are and what we are going through? And if God knows, then what does God will - what does God desire - to do about what we perceive to be our needs before God?

A study of scripture shows us that since the beginning of time, God has demonstrated that God knows exactly what we as humans are experiencing. It was out of this divine knowledge that God created the universe, and as a part of that creation, God created humanity. God who created all that is, knows everything about that which has been created. This is the very nature of God's omniscience.

God's omniscience simply means that God knows everything, about everything, wherever everything happens to be.

Furthermore, God's omniscience means that God not only knows what is happening in the present, but God knows what will happen before it happens. We are told by the apostle Paul that God foreknew the coming of Jesus Christ into the world. In other words, God knew that Jesus, God's Son, would come into the world even before Jesus was born as the incarnate Son of God over 2000 years ago.

This is also to say that God's knowledge is different, more multi-dimensional than what we experience as human knowledge. It has been discovered that human beings only remember (retain) about 10 percent of what we hear. That is why I would need to preach this same sermon, to the same people, at least 10 times for us to really get it.

But God's knowledge is far more comprehensive. God's knowledge is not merely cognitive and intellectual - as we have come to perceive human knowledge. God's knowledge of us is found in intimate, integral, and experiential dimensions, as well. God knows us in a spiritual way also.

The fact that God knows us means that God has the capacity to be involved with every aspect (every nook and cranny) of our lives. This means that God's holiness can be connected with the entirety of the human experience, and that God is concerned with the immensity of the human soul - our minds, our emotions, and our will.

God understands how and what we think – God realizes how and what we feel - and God knows how and what we desire. This - the nature of God's knowledge - God's omniscience - is what the psalmist is writing about in Psalm 139. The psalmist says:

> *"O Lord, you have searched me and known me. You know my sitting down, and my rising up. You understand my thoughts afar off..."*

What an affirmation of faith it is that God has searched us and known us. It appears that the psalmist could attest to the experiences of many of us. If you are like me, you've been through some times in life when it seems that there's nobody who understands your particular predicament.

Have you ever been there?
- Nobody understands the sickness that you're experiencing.
- Nobody understands the bills that you have.
- Nobody understands your problems on your job.
- Nobody understands the difficulties you're having with a loved one.
- Nobody understands that your children won't act like you think they should.
- (Young people) Nobody understands that your parents won't act like you want them to.

The song-writer put it this way in an old Negro spiritual:
Nobody knows the trouble I've seen
Nobody knows my sorrow...
Nobody knows the trouble I've seen
Glory Hallelujah...

Nobody seems to understand - nobody seems to know - and if they do know, they don't seem to really care about what you or I are going through.

But it's good to know that God knows. The psalmist was going through some things, but what he was trying to tell the faith community of his day, and what he affirms for us today, is that God knows.

This is important, because indeed there will be times in all of our lives when there seems to be nobody who knows or cares. The psalmist had to remind himself that:

- Before anybody knew his name - it was God who had covered him in his mother's womb.
- Before anybody knew his name - it was God who had fearfully and wonderfully made him.
- Before anybody knew his name - it was God who knew of his substance.
- Before anybody knew his name – it was God who knew of the potential and the possibility ahead in his life.

It's good to know that God knows. We share this affirmation today because the trials and tribulations of life are inevitable and real. Disappointment and discouragement are inevitable and real in this life. You can be on top of the world today, and down in the dumps tomorrow. You can think you know all there is to know, and have it all together, and then realize that you find yourself in the predicament that the great writer James Baldwin wrote about several years ago…"nobody knows my name…"

- I thought I was somebody, but nobody knows my name.
- I have a degree, but nobody knows my name.
- I've got a large 401K, but nobody knows my name.
- I've got a good job, but nobody knows my name.
- I drive a Lexus or a 'Benz, but nobody knows my name.

Yes, the reality is that - regardless of who we think we are - regardless of how big we think we've made it - regardless of how important somebody has made us feel - we all live on the brink of 'nobodyness'. We all live on the edge of obscurity, because we can never do enough to please everybody.

But, I've come to remind us that in the midst of our nobodyness, we are all somebody in the sight of God.

God knows. Yes, one song-writer said that "nobody knows the trouble I've seen". But I'm glad that another song-writer came along and talked about the ways of the Lord, and said:

> There's not a friend like the lowly Jesus
> No not one, no not one.
> There's not a time when he does not cheer us
> No not one, no not one.
> Jesus knows all about my struggles
> He won't rest until the day is done
> There's not a friend like the lowly Jesus
> No not one, no not one!

Chapter 14
THE POWER OF LOVE

> ***But I, through the abundance of your steadfast love, will enter your house. I will bow down toward your holy temple in awe of you. Lead me, O Lord, in your righteousness because of my enemies; make your way straight before me. (Psalm 5:7-8)***

It is clear throughout scripture that God's nature is love, and that God's divine intent is that humans live in love with one another. In Psalm 5, we find the first mention of the steadfast love of God. The Hebrew word for this steadfast love is *"chased"* – which is translated to mean the loving-kindness of God. This word *chased* is the same word that the psalmist used later to declare to God in a prayer, *"Lord, because your loving-kindness is better than life, yet will I praise you."* (Psalm 63:3)

Theologian and biblical scholar J. Clinton McCann asserts that *chased*, of all the Hebrew words, best describes the character of God because its meaning points to God's compassion, faithfulness, mercy, grace and love for us. *Chased* speaks to the power of the love that God has for you and me. It speaks to the omni-benevolence God – the notion that God's love is all encompassing – over all time and space.

As the book of worship for the people of Israel, the Book of Psalms served as a source of comfort, assurance and hope for an ancient people who persistently found themselves searching for the presence, provision and power of God.

The psalms were their songs, and the Psalter was their hymn book. These songs were their acts of praise and affirmations of faith in God. Amidst their wandering, alienation and separation from God – and often their alienation and separation from one another – the Israelites depended upon the psalms to bring meaning and hope to their lives. These were indeed their songs of faith, hope and joy – songs that reminded them time and again of the reality of the forgiveness, mercy, redemption and deliverance of their God.

Through slavery and oppression – it was the psalms that they looked to for encouragement. Through depression and even death, they depended on the psalms. Even in their difficulties in remaining faithful in worshipping the God of their ancestors – even amidst their idolatry and turning away from the Lord - it was the psalms that pointed them back to God.

These were their songs of Zion – songs for the day and the night. And so the Israelites would sing through the various and sundry vicissitudes of their lives –

- *My Lord, my Lord, why have you forsaken me?* (Psalm 22:1)
- *By the rivers of Babylon there we sat and wept when we remembered Zion... How can we sing the Lord's song in a strange land?* (Psalm 137:1-4)
- *I'd rather be a doorkeeper in the house of the Lord, than to dwell in the tents of wickedness.* (Psalm 84:10)
- *Yea though I walk through the valley of the shadow of death, I will fear no evil.* (Psalm 23:4)
- *I looked to the hills, from whence cometh my help? My help comes from the Lord.* (Psalm 121:1)

- *Weeping may endure for a night, but joy comes in the morning.* (Psalm 30:5)
- *If it had not been for the Lord on my side, where would I be?* (Psalm 124:1)
- *Let everything that has breath, praise the Lord.* (Psalm 150:6)

Indeed, it was the psalms that kept the Israelites when they needed to be kept, held them when they needed to be held, and pointed them to the reality of the presence of a loving and grace-filled God in their lives.

It has been suggested that any effective sermon should engage both the Bible and the newspaper. In reflecting on the matter of love – instead of drawing our insight from the newspaper, we turn here to the music of the late great soul singer, Luther Vandross. Several years ago, Vandross sang about the power of love. In his song, he sang:

> When I say goodbye it is never for long
> 'Cause I know our love still lives on
> It will be again exactly like it was
> 'Cause I believe in the power of love.

Any few minutes listening to popular radio would make it clear to us that "love" is a very important matter. Whether one's taste in music is Rhythm and Blues, or Easy Listening… whether one likes Hip-Hop, Jazz, the Blues, or Country and Western - love songs are everywhere. Whether one enjoys their music fast or slow – or somewhere in between – one only has to listen for a few minutes – to hear something about love.

Why this fixation with love? Perhaps it is because love has always been a matter of universal concern among God's people.

We want to find love, we want to be loved, we want to find those who we can love, and we want to know what love is (and what love is not). The irony comes in the fact that the more we see and hear love played out in the media – the more it seems that love is misunderstood and elusive in our contemporary world.

These are days when it seems that too many people are looking for love in all the wrong places, and in all the wrong ways. Look at the number of divorces, the preponderance of domestic abuse and violence, the burgeoning human trafficking of young girls and boys, and the number of those who find themselves in counterproductive relationships. Look at the number of Internet chat lines and dating services that continue to crop up.

Look at the number of people in our materialistic, consumer driven world who seem to find themselves unhealthily in love with their careers, their reputations, their houses and cars.

And in many ways, even in light of all of this talk about love, people today seem to be angrier than we ever have been. Look at the evening news. Fighting and hatred are everywhere in our midst - neighbors fighting neighbors... countries fighting countries... races fighting races... the rich against the poor... conservatives against liberals... Democrats against Republicans. Christians are even sometimes fighting other Christians.

And so it is in Psalm 5 that the psalmist speaks to the power of love – and not just any kind of love, but the steadfast love – the *chased* - of God. The psalmist declares, *"But I, through the abundance of your steadfast love, will enter your house."* The psalmist is affirming that God's steadfast love is abundant – and thus, God welcomes us into God's divine presence.

This should be good news for somebody who has been wondering whether or not they are loved by God. This should be good news for those who may have been searching for love in all

the wrong places. It is good to know that God is a loving God –
and that in fact God's very character – God's very nature - is love.
God is love.

Toward the end of his song, Luther Vandross reminded us
again of the power of love:

We've got love power
It's the greatest power of them all
We've got love power
And together we can't fall.

We've got the power of love! Ultimately this love power – this
steadfast love – this power of love – this *chased* - is expressed in
the person of Jesus Christ.   In the Book of John, we are reminded
of this love where it is written that *"...God so loved the world, that
God gave his only begotten son, so that whoever believes in Him
shall not parish but have everlasting life."* (John 3:16)

And if that doesn't help you, maybe the hymn-writer does:

I was sinking deep in sin
Far from the peaceful shore,
Very deeply stained within
Sinking to rise no more,
Then the master of the sea
Heard my despairing cry,
From the water lifted me
Now safe am I.

Love lifted me, love lifted me
When nothing else would help,
Love lifted me!

Chapter 15
SEEKING PEACE

Come, O children, listen to me. I will teach you the fear of the Lord. Which of you desires life, and covets many days to enjoy good? Keep your tongue from evil, and your lips from speaking deceit. Depart from evil and seek peace and pursue it. (Psalm 34:11-14)

(This sermon is an adaptation of a chapter in my book *Blessed are the Peacemakers; A Theological Analysis of the Thought of Howard Thurman and Martin Luther King, Jr.*, delivered at Emmanuel Episcopal Church; Baltimore, MD. in February 2009.)

These are days when various forms of violence seem to have permeated our conscience and pervaded our collective sense of being. Indeed, it would not be an overstatement to suggest that violence abounds.

There is evidence of violence all around us.
- Today, our nation continues to engage in two wars in the Middle East.
- The fastest growing industry in America is the prison industrial complex.

- America continues to be the most violent industrialized nation in the world.
- Cases of domestic violence against women and children seem to dominate our daily news.
- Too many aspects of our popular culture today, especially in our movies and in our music (including hip hop and rock), seem to glorify misogynistic behavior toward women.

A careful analysis of the biblical record indicates to us that violence was not God's original intent for the way that we would live our lives. The first two chapters of the book of Genesis describe a utopic world created in peace and harmony, a unified world perfectly ordered according to God's plan, a world with everything in right relationship - wholesome and good.

In Genesis 1:31, it is recorded: *"God looked at everything God had made, and found it very good."* This primordial peace was soon fractured, however, and conflict began. Over the course of time, Cain brought an offering to the Lord from the fruit of the soil, while his brother Abel, for his part, brought one of the best firstlings of his flock. The Lord looked with favor on Abel and his offering, but on Cain and his offering, God did not. Cain greatly resented this and was crestfallen...Cain said to Abel, *"Let us go out in the field."* When they were in the field, Cain attacked his brother Abel and killed him. (Genesis 4:3-5, 8)

And today, we find ourselves yearning for a return to the peace that God intended for us. The quest for peace, for a return to the uninjured wholeness of creation, is one of the deepest longings of humanity. It is a search for the essence and synthesis of human life, the harmony of all life's energies, and is based on the fundamental recognition that the divine intention is true; the world is indeed intended to be very good. A commitment to peace then is not just one task among the many of which humans are to engage. It is integral to the life that God intends for us to live.

The psalmist clearly articulates the task of humanity: *"seek peace and pursue it."* (Psalm 34:14) This is a theme that goes to the very heart of the identity of people of faith. It is a commitment inspired by scriptural witness and vision, and not only guides daily lives but challenges persons to do more in the search for community. It is a vision that gives meaning to everything we do as individuals.

What is the psalmist speaking of when he encourages the Israelites to seek peace and pursue it? The biblical concept of peace *(shalom, eirene)* is an amazingly comprehensive term. It includes salvation, wholeness, integrity and healing. Healthy relationships – interpersonal, cultural, economic, political, social and environmental - are implied. It is undivided integrity and oneness with God, inner peacefulness, and harmony in family, neighborhood, society and nations. Peace is the antithesis of disruption, alienation, separation, segregation, violence and war.

Biblical theologian Walter Brueggemann shares that the central vision of world history in the Bible is that all of creation is one, every creature in community with every other, living in harmony and security toward the joy and well-being of every other creature.[1] Brueggemann continues by pointing out that *shalom* – the Hebrew concept of peace, salvation and wholeness – is the substance of the biblical vision of one community embracing all creation. *Shalom* refers to all those resources and factors that make communal harmony joyous and effective.

This is what Isaiah meant when he wrote in the midst of the trouble and turmoil that Israel was going through that *"God will*

---

[1] Walter Brueggemann, *Living Toward a Vision* (New York: United Press, 1976), 15.

keep you in perfect peace, those whose eyes are stayed on him." (Isaiah 26:3)   Isaiah was talking about *shalom.*   And Paul encouraged and exhorted the Philippian church to *"rejoice in the Lord always. For the peace of God that passes all understanding will guard your hearts and minds in Christ Jesus."* (Phil. 4:7)

The kind of peace that Isaiah and Paul were talking about is the kind of peace that the world needs today.   It is a peace that is married with justice.   Dr. Martin Luther King, Jr. said that "true peace is not merely the absence of tension; it is the presence of justice." This is the essence of *shalom.*

With this understanding, it is easier to comprehend the exhortation that we are *to "seek peace and pursue it."* If, in fact peace is a state that is definable and attainable, if we are able to successfully seek peace, we are also encouraged to pursue it once it has been identified. The wisdom of the Bible knows and asserts that life is not simply peace or war, good or evil. Life does not consist exclusively of absolutes such as love or hate. Were peace merely the opposite of war, then the absence of war would bring peace. While shalom frequently connotes peace, which is usually understood to be the absence of war, the Hebrew concept enables us to appreciate realistically that there are degrees of peace; *shalom* is a balance and harmonization of forces that are sometimes contradictory and often beyond human control.

The people of Israel realized that they had not yet achieved wholeness. They were not fully what they ought to have been. They believed that they *once were* whole. They also believed that they would *once again* be whole – but that time was *not yet.* They saw the full reality of *shalom* as God's gift in the beginning, and that which they persistently yearned to attain. They saw *shalom* as God's eschatological gift at the end. Thus, *shalom* was an elusive reality for them. That is why Isaiah could speak of beating swords into plowshares, and also of beating plowshares into swords. *Shalom was in the beginning. It will be in the end. But it is not yet realized.*[2]

Perhaps it is the case that the psalmist is seeking to encourage each of us to become a peacemaker. Surely no one person can heal the pain of society where so many people suffer. But peace can be sought by looking for small ways to make a difference; and peace can be pursued regardless of how inconsequential the act of peacemaking may appear. This recognizes that cumulative acts of peacemaking positively affect the common fate and well-being of all human beings.

One rabbinical teaching intimates a perspective on sharing in acts of peacemaking:

Iron is strong, but fire melts it
Fire is strong, but water quenches it
The water is strong, but sun evaporates it
The sun is strong, but clouds can cover it
Clouds are strong, but wind can drive clouds away
Wind is strong, but man can shut it out
Man is strong, but fears cast him down
Fear is strong, but sleep overcomes it
Sleep is strong, yet death is stronger
But the strongest is the beautiful act,
For that survives death.[3]

One gesture may temporarily bind the hearts of persons, but that type of peace will hardly be permanent. One worship service, one hour of seeking God through prayer or study may enable

---

[2] William H. Shannon, *Seeds of Peace: Contemplation and Non-Violence* (New York: Crossroad, 1995), 108.
[3] This is a paraphrase from the Jewish Talmud.

persons to achieve spiritual solace and a sense of communion and unity, but such efforts can hardly make such an accomplishment permanent. It is evident that one good deed, one act of charity, cannot in and of itself bring total peace and healing amidst the world's ills. But when we persistently and communally strive after peace – when we seek peace and pursue it - we see God working, and *shalom* becoming real in our lives.

Perhaps, this is what Jesus was alluding to in one of his ethical teachings in the Sermon on the Mount where he said, *"Blessed are the peacemakers, for they shall be called children of God."* (Matthew 5:9) We are called to seek peace and to be peacemakers, for peacemaking is a means toward the blessing of God and the realization of the *beloved community.* We are called to heed the sentiments of Mohandas Gandhi, and be the change – the peace – we seek in the world.

In some of his final words as he appeared to his disciples after the resurrection, Jesus said, *"Peace be with you."* Christ, the Prince of Peace, calls the church and the world to peace, and beckons us to be peacemakers. The song-writer's words help us:

Let there be peace on earth,
And let it begin with me.
Let there be peace on earth,
The peace that was meant to be.
With God our creator,
Family all are we...
Let there be peace on earth,
And let it begin with me.

Chapter 16
THE VALUE OF THE VALLEY

Even though I walk through the darkest valley, I fear no evil; for you are with me, your rod and your staff, they comfort me. (Psalm 23:4)

One of the enduring reminders of the attacks of terror on New York City, Washington, DC and Pennsylvania on September 11, 2001 is the space in lower Manhattan that came to be known as "Ground Zero". In the aftermath of 9-11, Ground Zero came to describe the place of wreckage where there once stood the two architectural and economic marvels known as the World Trade Center buildings – or the "twin towers".

If the twin towers symbolized the possibilities of capitalism and prosperity, then Ground Zero symbolized the very reality of carnage and pain. If the twin towers spoke to the power and wealth of the western world, then it was at Ground Zero that we sensed the vulnerability and weakness that ultimately defines who we are.

For many, Ground Zero was merely an image that seemed to have traveled across our television screens too many times. But to understand the physical qualities of Ground Zero is to better comprehend the painful irony that resided there.

Only as one would visit Ground Zero – and set foot and eyes upon the site - was one truly able to discern the magnitude of the physical destruction that existed there. Where there once stood buildings over 100 stories high, which graced the New York City skyline - now one found a series of holes, pits and depressions in the ground.

At Ground Zero - in these holes – beneath the wreckage - there were reports that the remains of hundreds of human bodies lie unidentified and unrecognizable.   And in these pits and depressions one truly could sense the reality of despair and distress.   Underground   is   desperation   and   destruction. Underground is hopelessness and haplessness.   Underground - at Ground Zero - resides lost vision and unfulfilled dreams.

And if you know like I know, Blacks in America have been living in the existential reality of Ground Zero for a long time. Ground Zero - the GZ - is what philosopher Cornel West spoke of in his 1993 book, *Race Matters,* in terms of the nihilism of Black America.   Yes, a certain nihilism - a lovelessness, and meaninglessness, and emptiness, and hopelessness, and even nothingness seems to have pervaded our culture – and permeated our reality.

This is clearly seen in the fact that we have more black young men in prison than in college... it is seen in the fact that unemployment and underemployment remains rampant... it is witnessed in the fact that addiction and death ravages many of our city streets. A part of the tragedy of this nihilism - this Ground Zero existence - is that much of our reality, and many of our communities are perpetually mired in depression and in despair.

The writer of Job talked about this nihilism - this Ground Zero existence - when he reminded us that our *"days are but a few, and they are all filled with trouble."*

And here in the 23rd Psalm, we find that David was experiencing a similar type of nihilism - a Ground Zero existence. David was going through what he described as a valley experience. In fact it was not just any valley - David called it the *"valley of the shadow of death."* Somebody in another translation of the text called it *"Death Valley".* It was a valley filled with death and despair - there was no hope and no joy.

And David here needed some comfort and assurance in the midst of the valley experience in which he found himself, and so he wrote these words of assurance:

"Yea though I walk through the valley of the shadow of death, I will fear no evil. For thou art with me, thy rod and thy staff, they comfort me."

David was walking through a valley, and lest we take David's predicament too lightly, there are a few things we need to know about a valley. First, we realize that a valley is a *low place.* When one has arrived at the point of a valley, one has arrived at a low place, often the lowest point where one can be. (That's why geologists also refer to valleys as depressions.)

Secondly, at this lowest point, a valley is often a very *narrow place.* A valley is a place where you might find it difficult to see your way out. It is a confined space, a tight spot.

And thirdly, we know that a valley is usually a *dry place.* Geologists would indicate to us that a valley is a place through which an abundance of water may have once flowed, but now it is a dry place. And because it is a dry place, there is nothing there that can sustain human life.

This is the same predicament that the prophet Ezekiel found himself in when God spoke to him in "the valley of dry bones." It was a dry place with no hope, no joy, and no life.

But I've come to remind us that even amidst the troubles that we may experience in the valley - **there is value in the valley**.

What is the value of the valley? What can we learn in the midst of the valley? How might our valley experiences benefit us? There are a few things that we discover in the midst of the valley.

First, we discover something about the *value of vicissitudes*. Valley experiences teach us about the inevitability of vicissitudes in our lives. What are we talking about? Vicissitudes embody all of the ups and downs of life…the back and forth of life… the trials and tribulations and temptations of life.

We are reminded in the valley that we are all bound to go through some vicissitudes. John of the Cross characterized this as the "dark night of the soul". Ezekiel called it "the valley of dry bones". David called it here in Psalm 23, "death valley." He was going through some vicissitudes.

When you're at the end of your rope – with no hope and no joy - you're in the midst of some vicissitudes. Yes, we learn of the inevitability and value of vicissitudes in the valley, as they can really serve to make us stronger.

The second thing that we discover in the valleys of life is the *value of virtue*. God does not allow us to go through anything just for the sake of going through. But all that we experience is meant to make us stronger, better and wiser. I don't mean to glorify suffering and pain - valley experiences - but I've come to remind us that in our struggles God is always in the midst - desiring to make us stronger. Somebody has said that God never brings us 'to' anything that God won't take us 'through'.

Yes, there's virtue to be found even in the valley. There's virtue even at our points of despair and disappointment. There's virtue in our struggle because we become stronger. Martin Luther King, Jr. stated that "the true measure of a person is not how we act in times of comfort and convenience, but how we act in times of challenge and controversy."

Paul said in Romans 5 that we can *"glory in our suffering (tribulations) because suffering produces patience (endurance)... and patience produces experience ... and experience produces hope ... and hope does not disappoint us.*

When we are in the valley, when we are being tried and tested, we need to be reminded that God meets us at the place of all of our hopelessness and disappointment, and God wills to bring us through. There's virtue in the experiences of the valley.

Thirdly, in the valley, we learn the *value of vision.* In the valley we are reminded again that we are at our lowest point. It is there in the valley that we are in a depression.

And I've learned that at a low point, it does no good to look down, because to look down is to acknowledge that there is nowhere to go - to look down is to acknowledge that there is no hope, and no expectation of coming out.

And so, in a valley we realize that all we can do to survive and move forward is to look up. We have to look up to see God in our midst.

We're reminded of Peter - who one day saw Jesus walking on water. Peter couldn't believe his eyes - that Jesus - his friend was not just preaching and healing people - but that the Lord was now walking on water. And Jesus beckoned Peter to get out of the boat and walk on the water with him. Peter got out of the boat, but his natural inclination was to look down at the danger that the water at his feet presented. (He was scared!) But Jesus reminded Peter that he needed to keep looking forward and stay focused on the Lord. The only way that Peter was going to survive - and keep from drowning was to keep looking up - to keep his eyes on Jesus.

In the valley - just as a means of survival - we need to look up to God. In the valley, we need to know that our help is in the

Lord.   The Psalmist said, *"I looked to the hills, from whence cometh my help? My help comes from the Lord".*

Finally, after all that we've talked about, I've really just come to declare one thing. We ultimately realize, even in the valley, that *we've got victory!*

How could it be that we have victory even in the midst of the valley? Well, I consulted David again in the midst of his valley experience, and I found out that David did not start this song by talking about the valley, but David started by talking about the source of his strength. David declared that *"the Lord is my shepherd, I shall not want (I have everything I need)"*. I'm glad that David did not start out in the valley or stay in the valley. David realized that even though he was in the valley, the valley was not in him. David realized that even though he now found himself at his lowest point, this was not his final destination.

And so in the valley, David was able to declare:
"Lord, thy rod and thy staff, they comfort me."

Yes, David realized that God would watch over him in the valley, and so he also declared:
"Lord, you prepare a table for me in the presence of my enemies."

But David did not stop there.   He knew that the Lord's spirit was upon him, and so he declared:
"Lord you anoint my head with oil."

And David knew that even in the valley, God was not finished with him yet. So he declared:

>*"Surely goodness and mercy will follow me all the days of my life."*

I'm glad that in the valley, we have hope and life. In the valley, we have victory. In the valley, we have God's grace and mercy.

That's why some have come to call the Lord a "lily in the valley."

- In the valley, where there seems to be no life – Jesus is a life-giver.
- In the valley, where there seems to be no hope – Jesus is a hope-giver.
- In the valley, where there seems to be no joy – Jesus is a joy-giver.
- In the valley, he'll pick you up…

I was sinking deep in sin … far from the peaceful shore
Very deeply stained within …sinking to rise no more
But the master of the sea … heard my despairing cry
From the waters lifted me … now safe am I.
Love lifted me… Love lifted me.

When nothing else would help …Love lifted me!

Section Three
Joy and Celebration Songs

Chapter 17
AND YET THE MELODY LINGERS

> **By the rivers of Babylon – there we sat down and there we wept when we remembered Zion. On the willows there we hung our harps. For there our captors asked us for songs, and our tormentors asked for mirth, saying, "Sing us one of the songs of Zion!" How could we sing the Lord's song in a foreign land? (Psalm 137:1-6)**

Several years ago, the great soul band, "Earth, Wind and Fire" recorded a song in which they encouraged us in the title to "Sing a Song":

"When you feel down and out…
Sing a song…It'll make your day…
Here's a time to shout…
Sing a song… It'll make a way.
Sometimes it's hard to care…
Sing a song…It'll make your day…
A smile so hard to bear…
Sing a song… It'll make a way."

Indeed, there is something about the melodious music that we sing that serves to soothe our hearts, and lift our spirits. A good song can offer hope in despair and bring us joy in sadness. A good song indeed can make our day.

If there is anything that we - the people of the African Diaspora - share in common – it is that we are a singing people. This is to say that if there is any one thing that defines African people, it is our ability and willingness to sing. This has been one of our stamps, one of our marks - that we are a singing people.

Over one-hundred years ago, renowned sociologist, W.E.B. DuBois, in his classic work, *The Souls of Black Folk*, shared that black people have offered three significant, indelible gifts to American life as a whole – (1) the gift of the sweat and brawn; (2) the gift of the spirit; and (3) the gift of the story and song.

We are a people of the song – a people of the rhythm - a people of the beat. Whether in church or at the party, we have had a song to sing. Whether in the great cathedrals of the land or the best of concert halls, it has been well-known that African peoples are people of the song. Whether it was the spirituals or the blues, jazz or gospel, hip-hop or reggae, we have been a singing people.

What is impressive in travels to virtually any corner of the earth is that African people, wherever we are geographically located - and whatever our lot – are a singing people. Whether in Mutare, Zimbabwe, or Capetown, South Africa, or Sierra Leone on the western shores of the African continent, it is evident that we are a singing people. In the Caribbean or Central and South America, or in any neighborhood where we reside in the United States, it is clear that African people are a singing people.

The psalmist reminds us of the predicament of the Israelites in Psalm 137. Here they are, trapped in bondage by the rivers of Babylon… trapped in a foreign, strange land. And their captors asked the people of Israel to sing one of their songs of Zion. In their exile, they are provoked and prodded by their captors to sing one of their songs. And in their desperation, the Israelites responded by asking a question, *"How do we sing the Lord's song in a foreign land?"*

It is clear here that the Israelites found themselves in no mood to sing. How were they supposed to sing in the midst of adversity?   How were they supposed to sing amidst exile, oppression, separation and alienation?   They were in no mood to sing … trouble was all around them… they had no hope and no joy. How were they supposed to sing the Lord's song?

The turbulent and tempestuous nature of contemporary life can lead us to ponder this very same matter today. How do we keep singing… and keep worshipping… and keep praising the Lord… and keep trusting in Jesus in the midst of adversity?

How do we sing in the midst of abject poverty and virulent racism? How do we sing in the midst of suffering and sickness? How can we sing amidst violence and death? How do we sing when too many of our young people are dying on our streets? How do we sing the Lord's song in a strange land?

The Israelites' predicament teaches us something about singing the Lord's song. You see, it's easy to sing when life is rosy and cozy. It's not hard to sing when the bills are paid, and good health abounds. It's easy to sing amidst comfort and convenience.

But the true challenge of singing comes amidst the "strange land" situations of life. The challenge of singing comes when the nights are darkest, and even the days are dim - when there is little money in the bank…when it seems that loved ones have forsaken you… when it seems that you've done all that you can do to stand.

This is why we need to take time every now and then to be reminded of the importance of our song, and the need to keep singing. We will all face "strange land" situations in life. There will be times for all of us when we will sit beside the proverbial "rivers of Babylon."

We will all – at some point - face moments of feeling separated and segregated from God, and from one another - times of lostness and loneliness - times of desperation and disillusionment. And it is in these "strange lands" – on the "banks of Babylon" - that we need to be reminded and encouraged to keep on singing our song.

And we need to know that it's all right to ask from time to time, "How can we sing God's song?" It's all right to talk to the Lord, and ask "How?" For to ask the question indicates that we are still in conversation and relationship with God. This is an indication that we are still seeking and searching – praying and discerning - for the Lord to help us sing even though we may not feel like singing.

To ponder the question "How?" is to acknowledge - in the depths of our souls - that we may be bent, but we are not yet broken. We may be hurting, but we know that healing is possible. We may feel helpless and hopeless, but we know that if we hold on – our help is on the way. It's all right for people of faith to ask, "How do we keep on singing?"

The problem comes not in asking the question "How do we sing?" The problem comes when we stop singing altogether. The problem comes when we feel that there is no use in singing. The real predicament of faith lies at the point where we sense that we have been cut off from God, and that we may as well throw in the towel, give up, and stop singing. The problem really is evident when we stop singing the Lord's song.

And so, we have to keep on singing. We are reminded of those who sang the blues. Those like Billie Holiday, Bessie Smith, B.B King, Muddy Watters and Etta James were really helping us to understand that whatever the circumstance… whatever the predicament, we have to keep on singing. Whatever blows have been directed our way - we need to keep on singing.

And it's good to know that persons of faith like Dr. Thomas Dorsey, Dr. Charles Tindley, Dr. Mattie Moss Clark, Dr. Shirley Caesar, and Rev. James Cleveland were so inspired by God to take the blues, and turn it into some Good News. These persons of faith knew that despite the blues of life, it was incumbent upon people of faith to keep on singing the Lord's song.

And so Charles Tindley could sing:
When the storms of life are raging
(Lord) stand by me…
When the storms of life are raging
(Lord) stand by me…
When the world is tossing me
Like a ship upon the sea
Thou who rulest wind and water
(Lord) stand by me…

And then James Cleveland came along years later and declared:
I don't feel no ways tired
I've come too far from where I started from
Nobody told me that the road would be easy
I don't believe (God) brought (us) this far to leave (us)…

I'm glad that the melody lingers:
I sing because I'm happy
I sing because I'm free
God's eye is on the sparrow, and I know God watches me…
Keep singing!

Chapter 18
EXCELLENT

> ***O Lord, our Lord, how excellent is your name in all the earth.*** **(Psalm 8:1)**

As the song book for the people of Israel, the Book of Psalms served as a source of comfort, assurance and hope for an ancient people who often found themselves searching for the presence of God.

The psalms were their songs, and the Psalter was their hymn book, their book of worship and praise. Amidst wandering, alienation and separation from God, and often separation and alienation from one another, the Israelites depended upon the psalms to bring meaning and hope to their lives.

Through slavery and oppression – it was the psalms that they looked to. Through depression and even death, they depended on the psalms. Even in their difficulties in remaining faithful to worshipping the God of their ancestors, it was the psalms that pointed them back to God.

Indeed, it was the psalms that kept them when they needed to be kept, held them when they needed to be held, and pointed them to the reality of the presence of God in their lives. It is also evident throughout the psalms that the Israelites persistently sought to comprehend and articulate the very nature of God, and who God was for them. This striving is not unique to the Israelites. We, who are people of faith, are as St. Anselm intimated in the 11th and 12th centuries – perpetually seeking understanding within the context of our faith. Our journey is one of faith seeking understanding. It is one thing to have faith in God, but it is yet another thing to see more clearly the face of God amidst our faith. Our theological and spiritual task is to know who God is, so that we might grow more intimately in our relationship with God.

We live in a world where competition seems to be one of the prevailing marks of our life together. We compete with ourselves and we compete with each other. Most of us would agree that it is one of our objectives in life to be the very best that God calls us to become. We strive to succeed at whatever we do. We strive to win at the game of life.

This striving for success – this striving to be the best - tends to have one of two effects. The first is that it leaves many of us competing with our neighbors in ways that are not always helpful and healthy. Often, as we strive to be the best that we can be, others may be harmed along the way. If the truth is told, ours is a "dog-eat-dog" world. Charles Darwin – the social theorist – characterized this propensity among us as the "survival of the fittest." Too many people adhere to a life's philosophy of win at all costs, and as a result, there are inevitably winners and losers in the game of life.

I'm reminded of the old opening adage from the Wide World of Sports show that said that there is the "thrill of victory and the agony of defeat." The point was that all of the athletes who competed in any number of sporting events competed with an eye toward excellence and greatness, but some would experience the thrill of victory, while others would experience the agony of defeat. Some would be winners and some would be losers. Still excellence was always the striving.

The other result of our competition with others and with ourselves is a more positive one as we find the possibility of discovering what it is that God really intends for our lives – our purpose. Indeed, many of us never attain greatness in life because we are satisfied with just being good. In his book *Good to Great*, Jim Collins shares that one of the greatest hindrances of a person or organization becoming great is the satisfaction with being good. Gwande Atul in his book, *Better: A Surgeon's Notes on Performance*, shares that the difference between being good and being great is that greatness is being consistently good.

In this first song of praise in the Book of Psalms, David declares in Psalm 8, *"O Lord, our Lord, how excellent is your name in all the earth."*

It is interesting here that the psalmist states that the Lord's name is Excellent. Not good – but Excellent… not alright – but Excellent… not even very good – but the psalmist declares that Lord's name is Excellent. This speaks to the very nature of who God is. God's name is Excellent.

It is also interesting here that the psalmist directly addresses God. He begins by recognizing that we are children of a majestic, excellent God whose glory is manifested throughout the universe. David is awestruck by the evidence of God's unmatched greatness as seen in the works of God's hands, and he declares the Lord's name to be Excellent.

In Hebrew culture, the name that was given to a person spoke to the nature of who one was. One's name spoke to one's character. And so for David to declare that the Lord's name is Excellent was to speak about who the Lord is.

And we see that David does not stop at declaring that the Lord's name is Excellent. He goes on to wonder and marvel at the honored place given to human beings in the grand scheme of God's creation. David goes on to ask some questions in light of this. What are human beings that God is mindful of us? What are we that God has created us a little less than God? What makes you and me so important in the sight of God?

David stood in awe of the fact that God, whose name is Excellent, has God's mind on you and me. And likewise, you and I should be in awe at the thought – the notion – that God has God's mind on us. It's good to know that wherever we are, and whatever we do or don't do, God has God's mind on us. It's amazing – and should be good news - to know that God is mindful of us.

These are days when it is perhaps more important than ever for us to come to understand God's intent for our lives. And more than anything, what God wills for our lives is that which is excellent in accordance with the Lord's name. It's good to know that God desires the very best for our lives and for all of those we care about.

"O Lord, our Lord, how excellent is your name in all the earth."

God's name is Excellent!   As we think on these things, there is another one who God gave a name. The apostle Paul declared to the church at Philippi that the Lord's name was a name that was above every other name. That at the name of Jesus, every knee should bow and every tongue confess that he is the Lord! (Phil. 3)

What's in a name? It is also declared that there is no other name where men and women will be saved except the name of Jesus -

- At that name, angels bow.
- At that name, evil flees.
- At that name, sickness subsides.
- At that name, addictions cease.

- At that name, ways are made!

It's good to know that there's power, power, wonderworking power in God's excellent name! Indeed, as the psalmist declares, God's name is Excellent!

Chapter 19
IT'S TIME TO BLESS GOD

I will bless the Lord at all times; God's praise shall continually be in my mouth. My soul makes boast in the Lord; let the humble hear and be glad. O magnify the Lord with me, and let us exalt God's name together. (Psalm 34:1-3)

This week, we as a nation stand on the brink of remembering our common tragedy, that which has come to be known simply as '9-11'. We all have a story – a narrative – that places us in the context of this, our universal tragedy.

If the terror attacks of September 11, 2001 served any constructive purpose at all, they served to shake our collective conscience to the point where we all now seem (at least to some degree) to understand that our common destiny is intricately intertwined… and that we will either live together in peace - or we are bound to perish together amidst the violence that seems to so indelibly define our world.

The tragedy of 9-11 has taught us something about ourselves in another positive vain. Somehow, in its aftermath, people, for a moment, seemed to have embraced the importance of acts of kindness and compassion.

Somehow, we seized the moment, a piece of common humanity, and for that moment, we found it within ourselves to treat each other as human beings, regardless of our race or creed. It was just a moment in time - a few days. But for those days, politics as usual were not good enough for us, and America seemed to realize, for the first time in a long time, the communal capacity that we possess to actually love one another, treat one another with compassion, and understand the pain that we all share.

Indeed, one thing that we came to realize is that tragedy and terror are incumbent to the human experience. Many can attest to the fact that although it was a terrible tragedy – the death of nearly 3000 persons – and the uncountable others who have been - and continue to be - affected by the tragedy of 9-11… terror has afflicted the streets of America's cities for years.

Cities like Baltimore and Washington, DC have experienced the terror of drugs and violence – fratricide - where too many black folk have senselessly murdered too many other black folk. Many persons experience the living hell of the thousands of people who die on America's city streets every year. No, terror in this respect is not new to us.

Those in Jerusalem today - Palestinians and Jews - can attest to the terror that has been a part of their living reality for years. Our sisters and brothers in India and Pakistan live with the threat of nuclear terror. People in Afghanistan and in Zimbabwe, and in other parts of the world now find themselves mired in terror. Terror is not new.

Then, in the abyss of the tragedy of 9-11, we discovered the most important truth of all. This is a truth that I believe we had forgotten if we ever really knew it at all. It is a truth that was somehow lost in our strivings toward upward mobility… amidst commercialism, materialism and expanding stock portfolios…amidst the dot-coms that once were, but no longer are…amidst our newfound technological sophistication… amidst social division along race and class lines… amidst the partisan back-biting that has come to define our political reality.

Amidst all the things that had shaped and molded and defined us up to September 11, 2001, we had somehow, in no small way, lost a sense of our faith in God. We had gained the world, but had we, in the midst of our strivings toward success and prosperity, lost our collective soul? Yes, somehow, amidst the tragedy of 9-11, we discovered again that "it is time to bless God."

A recollection of the psalms helps us to recognize that trouble is not new to the human experience. No, the tragedy of terror is not new to our world. In fact, these songs, songs like Psalm 34, were typically written and sung within the context of real life experiences – real tragedy and terror... real wars and rumors of wars... real death and despair.

Tragedy was as incumbent to Israel's experience, as it is to ours.
- We remember that David said in another place, *"Yea though I walk through the valley of the shadow of death, I will feel no evil."* He was dealing with tragedy.
- In another song, the Israelites sat by the rivers of Babylon and pondered their plight, *"How can we sing the Lord's song in a strange land?"* They were dealing with tragedy.
- And yet somewhere else, the psalmist lamented, *"My God, my God, why have you forsaken me."* He was dealing with tragedy.

This is the context in which David would sing this song: *"I will bless the Lord at all times."*

One of the ironies of David's blessing God was that he made up in his mind that he was going to bless God - even in the midst of difficult times – at all times.

What I've found out is that a lot of people find it easy to bless God in good times - when the bills are paid...when everybody is healthy... and everyone seems to be getting along. But the true test of blessing God comes in times of challenge and controversy.

Here, David teaches us something that can help us in our most difficult times. David said that he would bless the Lord at all times - even in the midst of the tragedy and terror that had invaded his life.

- Tragedy incumbent in broken family relationships.
- Tragedy in the midst of trying to lead a nation.
- Tragedy amidst enemies on his left and on his right.

Here in Psalm 34, David seeks refuge - safety in the Lord - from King Saul who is trying to take is life. Amidst the terror that has affected all of us anew...amidst the terror that we now recollect, comes a profound affirmation. Amidst all that has occurred around us and may occur in our future, I've come to remind us that, "It's now time to bless God."

- It's time to acknowledge that God is God all by Godself.
- It's time to recognize that God calls us to nothing less than to *love kindness, and to do justice, and to walk humbly.* (Micah 6:8)
- It's time to remember that God spoke through King Solomon, and said, *"If my people, who are called by my name, will humble themselves and pray, and seek my face, and turn from their wickedness, I will hear their cry and heal the land."* (2 Chronicles 7:14)

Why do we need to bless the Lord today? (Let me offer a few reasons.)

- We need to bless God because *"greater is He that is in us, than he that is in the world."*
- We need to bless God because there is an indelible… unquenchable …undeniable strength that comes in the unity of God's people.
- We need to bless God because perfect love – God's love – casteth out all fear.
- We need to bless the Lord because we know that as people of faith - come what may – God will take care of us.
- We need to bless God, because God *"inhabits the praise of His people who bow down before Him."*

I don't know about you … but I've decided that I want to be like David. David said,

"*I will bless the Lord at all times, God's praise will continually (always) be in my mouth.* "

I've come to remind us that something happens when we bless God.

- When nations bless God…nations are exalted.
- When families bless God…families stay together.
- When churches bless God…they begin to grow.
- When praises and blessings go up - God begins to shower down blessings.

It's time for us to bless God.

- Times may be difficult right now…but keep blessing God.
- There may be some difficult days ahead…but keep on blessing God.

- Regardless of the circumstances...we've got to keep blessing God.

Because Jesus said, *"I, if I be lifted up from the earth, I will draw all people unto me..."*

It's time to bless God!

Chapter 20
IT'S A DONE DEAL (GOD DID IT FOR ME)

*I will thank you forever, because of what you have done.
In the presence of the faithful I will proclaim your name,
for it is good. (Psalm 52:9)*

We live in times of tremendous uncertainty in our world. Our lives are filled with uncertainty as to what the future holds for us… filled with uncertainty about the economy… uncertainty about our jobs (for some of us)… often even uncertainty about our faith in God.

There are a couple of observations that we can make (today) about uncertainty. First, when we are uncertain, we have the tendency to fall into doubt. Yes, when we are uncertain, we tend to doubt whether those things that may have appeared to be certain are certain for us after all. When we are uncertain, we tend to harbor doubt as to whether situations and circumstances are the way we thought they were, or ought to be.

Where things once seemed so certain for us, where life for a time may have appeared to be rosy and cozy, where our life-situation may have looked like one filled with only comfort and convenience, we now wonder and then we begin to doubt whether things can ever be the way we want them to be.

A second observation is that the results of our doubts are our worries. We begin to worry. We worry about things at home. We worry about our children. We worry about our husband or wife. We worry about our boyfriend or girlfriend. We worry about our job. We worry about neighbors. We even worry about the dog and cat. We worry about the things we have and the things we don't have. Our lives are filled with worry.

Surely, there are some problems too big for us... some situations that are too difficult and complicated for us to handle on our own. Amidst this reality, people today need something and somebody in which to place their confidence... something and somebody in which to find certainty. In what and in whom can we put our trust and place our faith?

The question for us is, "what is the remedy for people of faith to our uncertainties, our doubts and our worries?" What recourse and remedy do God's people have to worrying about what may or may not happen in our lives tomorrow?

Well, as a prescriptive to our uncertainty, we go to Psalm 52:9. Hear these words of comfort and encouragement from David:

> *"(Lord) I will thank you forever, because of what you have done. In the presence of the faithful I will proclaim your name, for it is good."*

As we reflect upon the life of David, we recall that David had experienced some ups and downs in his life. A shepherd boy in his youth, David would eventually be led into battle with the Philistine giant, named Goliath. David defeated Goliath, and went on to be blessed by God to become the king of Israel.

And yet despite all of his success, David continued to experience difficulties in his own life and in his walk with God. We encounter David's predicament throughout the many psalms that he wrote. On one account David would declare:

> *"Lord, because your lovingkindness is better than life, I will praise you."* (Ps. 63:3)

Then he would be led to write:
"*Lord, have mercy on me according to your loving-kindness.*"
(Ps. 51:1)

On another occasion David writes:
"*I will bless the Lord at all times; God's praise shall continually be in my mouth.*" (Ps. 34:1)

And the next moment he asks:
"*My God, my God, why have you forsaken me?*" (Ps. 22:1)

In another instance, David declares:
"*O Lord, our Lord how excellent is your name in all the earth.*" (Ps. 8:1)

And then David utters:
"*Yea though I walk through a valley of the shadow of death...*"
(Ps. 23:4)

David had gone through some things:
- For every victory, there seemed to be a vicissitude.
- For every triumph, there was a trial.
- For every battle won, there was a Bathsheba in his life.
- For every sign of David's faithfulness, there were symbols of failure and fallenness.

And aren't we often like David?
- For all the times that we are faithful to God, aren't there just as many moments that we find ourselves lacking faith?

• For every time that we are certain of God's presence, aren't there just as many instances of uncertainty for us?

• For all the times when we can rise to the occasion in life without any doubt or fear, aren't there just as many moments when we are filled with doubt in our hearts?

• And for all the instances when we are able to give our burdens to the Lord, for all the times when we are able to let go and let God, for all cases when we find it within ourselves to cast our cares on Jesus, aren't there those times when we let our problems worry us … depress us … give us the blahs and the blues?

Many of us find a kindred spirit in David. How do we know?

Business for many psychologists, psychotherapists, psychoanalysts and psychiatrists is booming. The pharmaceutical industry is booming – it seems that people are popping pills for everything – to stay awake... to go to sleep... for anxiety…. for energy… for depression… to control mood swings.

People are filled with uncertainty, doubt and worry. Many find themselves on the brink of brokenness in life. Many are experiencing trouble at home… trouble at school… trouble on the job… trouble with relatives… trouble with friends. Nations are fighting nations... neighbors are at odd with neighbors. We experience ups and downs… trials and tribulations… virulence and volatility. And the more we look to God, the more difficult it often seems for us to discover the Lord in a real way in our lives.

Well, I'm glad that David offers us a remedy for our ups and downs. David offers us some words of encouragement and hope for our moments of discouragement, uncertainty, doubt and worry.

David declares:

"Lord, I will praise you forever, because of what you have done."

Another translation says: *"Lord, I will praise you, for you did it."*

And so, how does David's affirmation help us today? What can we feed upon here that can help us in our moments of weakness, uncertainty, doubt and worry? How can David's words help to strengthen us for the journey ahead?

First, we discover through David that ours are to be lives of *perpetual prayer and persistent praise.* One thing that distinguishes this present age from ages past is that we are far less apt to pray and praise God than generations in the past were. God has become - for too many of us - a God of convenience. God is a secondary player – second fiddle… a supporting actor – in many of our lives - until we really need the Lord and find ourselves in trouble.

What David was conveying – not only through his words, but through his life - is that God has already made provision for all aspects of our lives. It is through the disciplines of *perpetual prayer and persistent praise* that we connect with God, and allow God to work in our lives.

Somebody made it plain when they declared – "When praises go up, blessings come down."

Second, David was also reminding us in Psalm 52:9 that God *is perpetually present.* Persons over the ages have learned to trust God because they have come to realize that God is perpetually present.

- From Egypt to Canaan, the Israelites came to know that God was *perpetually present.*

- From the shores of Africa to these American shores, persons of the African Diaspora have come to realize that God has been *perpetually present* for us.
- From the country cotton fields to city factories, God has been *perpetually present* for us.

And so we are confident today that whatever we need, wherever we go, whatever we do, whomever we meet, God is *perpetually present*. In our rising in the morning and lying down at night, God is *perpetually present*. On our jobs, in the car, on planes, trains and buses, God is *perpetually present*.

Third, we discover through David that in our faith in God there is *pervasive power*. We know that in God there is power. We utter it in the affirmation of our faith:

"I believe in God the father almighty, the maker of heaven and earth."

The song-writer said it another way:

"There's power, power wonder-working power in the blood of the Lamb."

There's *pervasive power* in Jesus. When I think about Jesus, I think about power. The Lord's whole purpose was to demonstrate the power of God. Jesus was born in a manger... raised in Nazareth... and baptized in the Jordan. He went about demonstrating the *pervasive power* of God. Jesus healed the sick, and he raised the dead, and he fed the hungry, and gave sight to the blind.

I'm glad that Jesus had, and he has *pervasive power*. Jesus has all power in his hands, and he gives us power to walk right…power to talk right…. power to live right…power to love right.

David said, *"I will praise you, because of what you have done."* "Lord, you did it for me!"

What was this "it" that David was talking about? What had the Lord done for David? What has the Lord done for you and me? Lest we forget, I think it's helpful every now and then to pause and to take inventory (to take stock) of what the Lord has done for us?

God has done it for you and me. What is this "it"? What has the Lord done for us?

- God woke us up this morning and started us on our way.
- God provided for all our needs… put clothes on our backs… food on our tables… shelter over our heads.

God did it!

God loved us… forgave us… pardoned us from our sins… highly favored us… helped us when were in trouble.

God did it!

- God redeemed us, reformed us, and reshaped us.
- God remade us, remolded us, and restored us.
- God reconciled us, renewed us, and reclaimed us.
- God renamed us, and revived us.

God did it!

"I will thank you forever, because of what you have done."

And, I've come to remind us that because of what God has already done for us, **"It's a Done Deal!"**

Chapter 21
THIS IS A NEW DAY

This is the day that the Lord has made; let us rejoice and be glad in it. (Psalm 118:24)

In every age and every generation it is the task of the church to reflect upon what it has been, what it is, and what it is that God calls us to become.

Remembrance - for persons of faith in ancient times - was often an opportunity to recollect on the past – a time of reminiscence about what God had done in their lives. But remembrance was also a time of looking to the future with expectancy as to what God was about to do in and for the people. The Greek notion of *anamnesis* is most evident in this kind of remembrance – where we are both looking back at the past and looking forward to the future.

Some theologians have suggested that the church is a people of both the "right now" and the "not yet" – or the yet to be. This is the hope that we share in Christ. Ours is a faith that is yet being fulfilled in this life. We are a pilgrim people, on a journey of faith and discipleship to those places and spaces where God is yet leading us.

And so it is that we come today. We come reflecting upon the past – what God has done in and through and for us – and looking to the future to see what God is about to do.

As those of ancient times would gather to remember, each of us here today has a story to tell of how God has met us here. And so it is that we gather with memories of the past and hopes for the future.

This is the encouragement that we find in the words of the psalmist, who said:
"This is the day that the Lord has made, let us rejoice and be glad in it."

Eugene Peterson in *The Message* reframes (remixes) this passage in this way:
"This is the very day GOD acted. Let's celebrate and be festive."

Indeed, we can rejoice and celebrate and be glad today knowing that God has created a new day for us, with new possibilities. We can rejoice and celebrate and be glad because we are confident that God offers us new challenges and opportunities – new and exciting ways of being in ministry. Indeed, ours, as the prophet Jeremiah once declared, is a future filled with hope. (Jeremiah 29:11)

Endings and beginnings are never easy – for they insinuate change. Amidst the reality of change, we often find ourselves pondering the question," Is the cup of life half empty or is it half full?"

I want to suggest that for people of faith, the cup of life is always both half empty and half full. With change – with new beginnings - comes new opportunities and challenges, new possibilities and promise, new and exciting ways for us to experience God in our future. We are a people of hope – and indeed this is a new day.

And so I believe the words of the great song-writer Brian Wren are appropriate for us today:

This is a day of new beginnings
Time to remember and move on
Time to believe what love is bringing
Laying to rest the pain that's gone.

Then let us with the Spirit's daring
Step from the past and leave behind
This is a day of new beginnings
Our God is making all things new.

In faith we'll gather round the table
To taste and share what love can do
This is a day of new beginnings
Our God is making all things new.

It remains our awesome task, as the church, to live faithfully and hopefully into the new day that God offers us. And it will be our faith and hope in God that will sustain us, strengthen us, encourage us, and lead us into the future with hope.

Indeed, it has been faith that has sustained you and me, and this same faith will be with us into the future. Another song-writer intimated that:

God (has been) our help in ages past,
(and God is) our hope for days to come.
(God has been) our shelter in the storms,
and (God is) our eternal home.

O that God would continue to lead us and guide us into this new day. And O that we would look to the days ahead with trust and faith in God who has created us.

I do not know how long 'twill be
Or what the future holds for me
But this I know,
If Jesus leads me
I'll get home someday. (Tindley)

Chapter 22
THANK YOU!

> *Praise the Lord! O give thanks to the Lord, for God is good; for God's steadfast love endures forever. Who can utter the mighty doings of the Lord, or declare all God's praise? (Psalm 106:1-2)*

It has been suggested that there is an infectious disease that is permeating our land. It is the disease of ingratitude. We live in an age where many people have forgotten how to say "thank you." Ingratitude has overtaken us.

If you know like I know, there is a certain irony that can be found here… in that we are more blessed than we have ever been in the history of civilization. We are blessed with technological advances and material things about which our fore parents could have only dreamt.

Many of us have finer homes, and larger cars, and more expensive clothing than we ever thought we should or could possess. Many of us are blessed to be more educated and to have better jobs, and some of us even have a few more dollars in the bank than those who came before us. We're blessed.

But still many people are infected with this disease of ingratitude. For some reason many people are ungrateful… many people don't know how to say "thank you."

I remember growing up, and being taught, as one of the first lessons of life, how to say "please" and "thank you." It was engrained into our very beings as young people that if you wanted somebody to do something for you… you'd first say "please."

And once somebody was kind enough to do something for you, however small or large the act, the appropriate response was to say "thank you."

Now it seems that many people think that it is their right and entitlement that somebody would do something for them. They have the audacity – the nerve – the unmitigated gall – to ask without first saying "please," and to receive without then saying "thank you." Indeed, ingratitude is in our midst.

In Psalm 106, we find the psalmist reminding those who would hear with these words, *"O give thanks to the Lord, for God is good, for God's steadfast love endures forever."*

This is a word of reminder to the faithful. In order that their faith might be well-founded and properly grounded, in order that their hope and perspective might be sustained, the psalmist offered the people a lesson in thanksgiving. In order to improve their aptitude for praise and enhance their attitude of gratitude, the psalmist here offers words of instruction as to the conditions under which the believers of his day were to render their appreciation, and say "thank you" to the Lord.

Praise and thanksgiving are the foci of this psalm. The psalmist calls for thanksgiving to God, to sing and tell of God's wonderful works, and give glory to God's name… to praise the Lord for God is good. This is a reminder to all of us, for indeed, some people never seem happy or satisfied. In one of his New Testament studies, William Barclay tells of a man who saved a young boy from drowning. When he returned the boy to his mother, she asked, "Where's his cap?" Too often we see the glass as half empty rather than more than half full. Rather than being appreciative of the things that we do have, we are too often apt to complain about what we don't have.

The psalmist's words of encouragement are that we are to give thanks to the Lord for God is good, and God's steadfast love endures forever.

In a similar word of admonition and encouragement, the apostle Paul wrote to the church at Thessalonica and said, *"In everything give thanks, for this is the will of God concerning you."* (1 Thess. 5:18)

What Paul was saying to the congregation is that the zenith of Christian conduct is to be able to say "thank you." *"In everything, give thanks,"* Paul says.

Here, in Thessalonians we find that the apostle Paul was en-route to Rome with a layover in Corinth when he wrote his first letter to the young church at Thessalonica. Paul was aware that the church there would have its ups and downs, its risings and fallings. It is apparent, above all else, that the people, in the midst of whatever they were going through, had forgotten how to say "thank you" to the Lord.

And so Paul says that they were to give thanks in all things. Herein lies the challenge of faith and life. For, if we are to follow Paul's instruction, we will develop the capacity and practice of giving thanks for the good and the bad of life. We will be able to give thanks in ups as well as in downs, in joy and pain, in sunshine and rain, in life and in death, in triumphs and in trials.

Giving thanks in all circumstances is really a test of our Christian character. Dr. Martin Luther King, Jr. said it best when he shared that 'the true measure of our character is not how we conduct ourselves in times of comfort and convenience, but how we deal with challenge and controversy."

If we affirm what the psalmist wrote centuries ago, we know that God is good. The psalmist says that we are to *"give thanks to the Lord, for God is good."* This speaks to the very nature of who God is. The Lord is good. This is the acknowledgement of the omni-benevolence of the Lord, that the Lord is good in all God's ways.

- From the rising of the sun, to the going down of the same, God is good.
- In ups and downs, God is good.
- In joy and even in sadness, the Lord is good.
- In times of prosperity and even in times of need, the Lord is good.

O give thanks to the Lord, for God is good!

I'm reminded of the story of a businessman, who one Thanksgiving, while watching a football game, reflected on his life and thought of all the people who had been influential in helping him become who he was. He decided to write each person a thank-you card telling her or him of his gratitude for their influence on his life.

His fourth grade teacher quickly came to mind for insisting that he and his classmates strive for excellence in every endeavor. She pounded it into her students, be it regarding homework, tests or class projects. So he sent her a thank-you note.

One day, just after the New Year, he received a return letter from his former teacher. She apologized for not replying sooner, but stated that his letter had taken some time getting to her, since she had moved in with her daughter after retiring from teaching grade school for sixty-six years. She told him how thankful she was to have received his card and how it cheered her to find out he had learned so well his lessons in excellence. She went on to say that in her sixty-six years of teaching, this was the first thank-you card she had ever received, and how grateful she was that he had taken the time to remember her.

O give thanks to the Lord, for God is good, and God's steadfast love endures forever. Oh, that people of Christian faith would find a way to say "thank you" to God for all that God has done for us.

When I think of the goodness of Jesus
And all that he's done for me
My soul cries out, Hallelujah,
I thank God for saving me!

ABOUT THE AUTHOR

C. ANTHONY HUNT

A native of Washington D.C., Rev. Dr. C. Anthony Hunt currently serves as the Senior Pastor of Epworth Chapel United Methodist Church in Baltimore, MD, and as Professor of Systematic, Moral and Practical Theology and Permanent Dunning Distinguished Lecturer at the Ecumenical Institute of Theology, St. Mary's Seminary and University in Baltimore. He also teaches at Wesley Theological Seminary in Washington, DC, United Theological Seminary in Dayton, OH and at the Graduate Theological Foundation in Mishawaka, IN, where he is a faculty Fellow and E. Franklin Frazier Professor of African-American Studies.

He is a graduate of the University of Maryland, and holds advanced degrees from Troy State University, Wesley Theological Seminary and the Graduate Theological Foundation. Additionally, he has completed post-graduate studies at St. Mary's Seminary and University, Baltimore, MD; the Center of Theological Inquiry, Princeton NJ; the University of Oxford, UK, and the Institute of Certified Professional Managers, James Madison University, Harrisonburg, Va.

Anthony is the author of seven books including, *Blessed are the Peacemakers: A Theological Analysis of the Thought of Howard Thurman and Martin Luther King, Jr.* (2005), and *My Hope is Built: Essays, Sermons and Prayers on Religion and Race, vol. 2* (2011), and over 85 articles and chapters on matters pertaining to religion and society. He is also an active blogger at www.newurbanminstry.blogspot.com.